The Executive Secretary Guide to Creating an Internal Assistant Network

Cathy Harris

Marcham Publishing

© Cathy Harris 2017

All rights reserved.

ISBN 978-0-9957000-4-8

Cover image by missimoinsane
http://missimoinsane.deviantart.com/

Contents

Preface

In the infant stages of our assistant network we battled to get both management and the assistant community to buy into the concept, but once we got organized, prepared a value-added proposal, and set objectives and goals for ourselves, we were able to move forward successfully. Success didn't happen overnight and it took a lot of hard work, dedication, commitment and team effort to bring us to where we currently are. However, continuing our success will take even more effort and consistent commitment.

In this book I would like to share my experiences with you, as well as to give you the tools to either create or improve on your own internal assistant network. I have witnessed how assistants have battled to survive on their first day in the office, and those who never quite knew what to do and the correct processes to use. I myself had to find out the hard way, and the hard way meant time wasted seeking the right information and connecting with the right people. Having an internal network is also about having a passion for what you do, understanding the different personalities amongst the assistant community and growing your personal leadership ability.

The ideas and suggestions within this guide can be adjusted to suit your own organization's culture and style – some ideas will work, some may not be applicable – but all in all the basic foundation is provided and it will be up to you and your team to make it successful. My hope is that this book will inspire you, encourage you and provide you with an opportunity to develop the leader in you.

1

Introduction

It is often stated that when the need arises the deed is done! This sentiment is true for many areas of life and in particular when it comes to the important role the management assistant plays in everyday tasks and projects. The role of the assistant has evolved from that of tea maker and minute taker to one of strategic partner with the executive and management team. Yes, the role has evolved, and just as the leadership builds a common strategy together as peers, so too the assistants should do likewise.

The time has come for us to change the way we think, to review how we do things, and to ask ourselves what the best course of action is to make things happen fast, efficiently and within the operational parameters of the organizations we work for.

Without question we have to move in sync with changing business styles, pressures and demands, coupled with the increase in workload and the expectation of shorter turnaround times. It has become increasingly necessary for management assistants to explore ways to change the way tasks and projects are achieved and to figure out how to effectively access processes, people and networks in the organization, in order to get the job done as quickly and efficiently as possible.

The problem is that we often don't have the right networks around us to be able to collaborate, connect, educate and share knowledge, skills and resources. Companies lose thousands of hard-earned bucks annually because they follow traditional routes when sourcing training for us, updating resource tools and implementing processes that often don't work, while right under their noses a cost-saving and innovative approach is waiting to be exploited.

And what is this innovation? It's simple. The creation of internal assistant networks within organizations is a perceptive, innovative resource tool to improve communication, create standards, provide training and development initiatives, and give the assistant the opportunity to always be ahead of the game.

The assistant is the one person who manages the manager, the person who has to use processes developed or chosen by those who don't actually use them on a daily basis, the person who needs to know everything about the organization. Yet the assistant seldom gets the opportunity to network, because networking is perceived to be more of a social event than a powerful harvesting of connectors and collaborators. Internal assistant networks provide the opportunity to bring a plethora of information and skills together for use by anyone who needs it.

An internal network will provide access to essential resources required by the assistants for mandatory operational procedures pertinent to our role, and a fair and equitable opportunity to be accountable for our profession by actively participating in the internal network committee, and the initiatives derived from it, in a positive and constructive manner.

This book was written to share with you and your assistant community a resource tool that will be of significant value not just to your organization and its management teams, but on a personal developmental level as well.

This said, a network requires ongoing maintenance, commitment and dedication from those who are both passionate about their profession and willing to create a legacy. In plain English, it will take a few kick-ass assistants to make it happen. The question is, are you one?

This book will provide you with absolutely everything you need to know about internal networks, what they are, how they can be managed and maintained and how you can set up one that will be both functional and fun!

2

What is an Internal Network?

What is an internal assistant network, and why would we want one for our organization?

The answer is simple. An internal assistant network is a group of dedicated and passionate assistants that share a variety of skills, values and role functions. It requires assistants who are connected together to excel at optimizing communications, empowering each other, creating high standards, being professional and respectful, and who are committed to making a tangible contribution, outside of their normal job descriptions, to add value to their organizations, their peer groups and themselves.

Yes, these are special individuals, game changers, role models and legacy makers, and if you are reading this, you have the potential to be one of them.

But let's take a more holistic view of what it really is and how you and your peers can implement this concept inside your organization. We will discover that assistant networks already exist and are being run successfully in different formats across the globe. We will also be sharing compelling case studies as food for thought.

What is an internal network?

Networking in itself means linking up, collaborating, sharing opinions, ideas and experiences, interacting with discussion and debate, and taking action on these shared ideas. An internal assistant network shares the same concept with one focus in mind, to get all the assistants within an organization:

- to share and implement the same operational standards and to work on enhancing current solutions,

- to be contributors towards processes they are the end users of, thereby giving valuable input and recommendations to make these processes work better,

- to create a powerful and dynamic collaboration between themselves that builds strong mutual respect,

- to create cost saving initiatives and projects that benefit the organization's bottom line,

- to build strong leadership skills within their peer groups,

- to create opportunities for the assistants to develop on a professional and personal level,

- to add priceless value to the support provided to the assistants' managers and teams.

No matter which way we cut it, an internal assistant network is a powerful resource for organizational good.

An internal network is **not**:

- A forum to log complaints about your managers, co-workers or peers,

- An opportunity to host Tupperware parties and social events just for fun,

- The hosting of social events that serve little purpose to the organisation or the assistants,

- And it is certainly not a club for a select few!

Why would you want an internal network for your organization?

When we isolate ourselves from the opportunity of networking, we also deprive ourselves of the opportunity to learn and grow, we miss the ability to gain more insightful knowledge of skills we never knew existed, and we never really experience the effects that positive changes in how we do things can bring for us.

At the same time this negative behaviour denies our managers better and more efficient support. Taking a narrow-minded approach to collaborating and networking harms you and your management team. So, as you can see, there is a huge need for organizations to embrace an innovative concept and a new way of working by implementing an internal network.

So there are plenty of great reasons to have an internal network, but I want to focus on those initiatives which directly impact the best practices for our organizations. The first of these are operational standards.

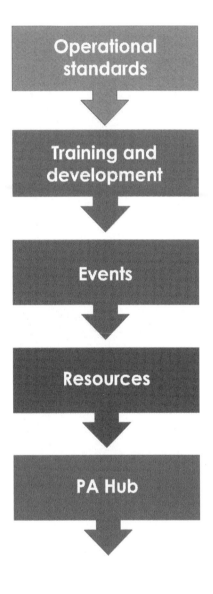

Initiative No. 1: To set operational standards

Currently, in many companies, assistants distance themselves from each other, work independently from each other, stay cooped up in their own space, display territorial tendencies, and take offence at the mere thought of including others' ideas or suggestions into their closed circle, and, even worse, reject any idea that there are things they need to learn. We have become our own worst enemies. We tend to set our own standards, create our own little processes, and when we are approached to participate in positive change, we go into deep denial and disregard the suggestion as a conspiracy against us.

It is now time to think about the real reasons why organizations have standards, and why we as assistants need to be part of the process. With the help of an internal network we can collectively agree on our standards and make them available for use by all the assistants in the organization, thereby creating a forum where these standards can be updated and maintained. How this is accomplished will be explained further on in this book.

By setting standards, not just in our work processes, but in the way in which we operate as an organization, we create a very powerful branding tool. Having standards set for everything we do, the way in which an email signature is laid out, how we process the payment of goods, type up our minutes, communicate internally and everything else in between, gives our managers comfort that we are ALL doing the right things in the right manner.

Standards help us to fine tune our personal performance and contributes to managing the many risks associated with not having standards in place, for example ensuring updated company letterheads displaying current directors and other organizational details which, if incorrect, could have resulting legal implications. Standards embed best practices into your company. Embrace them!

Sometimes we feel that if we asked for help from another assistant, it would expose us as being weak, stupid, uninformed and out of touch. Little do we realize that it is actually the other way round, that when we don't ask for help we are actually exposing ourselves as weak (as we don't have the self-confidence to ask for help), and when we don't ask for help we remain uninformed and out of touch, yet we continue to do things our own way, believing it to be the only way.

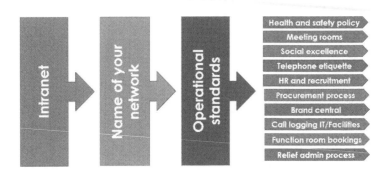

What are these operational standards?

Every organization has various processes in place and each one of these processes require standards. The idea is that all **operational standards** that assistants use frequently will be accessible on the organization's intranet site, or a website set up for the Assistant Network.

'Operational standards' is the first of five initiatives which I will be sharing with you in this book. Let's look at all the things that fall under operational standards. They are all outcomes or activities accompanied by rules and protocols, which need to be accessed and used by us on a daily basis. My list is merely an example; you can think about what other outcomes you could add to your own intranet folder.

The idea is to have all related information, protocols and rules linked to this initiative so that assistants can easily access the correct process and apply it in their tasks.

- Health and safety policy

- Meeting rooms (rules, booking system, venue finding, seating, catering etc.)

- Social excellence initiatives

- Telephone etiquette (company standard answering, voice messaging, call forward)

- Recruitment and HR

- Procurement processes (stationery ordering tools, vendors, account processes)

- Brand central (letterheads, templates, email banners, etc.)

- IT call logging system

- Function room bookings

- Relief assistant process

These are all operations functions that require a standard set of outcomes in line with your organization's operational policies. These initiatives are those where we as assistants need to accept the responsibility of ensuring we follow the standard, and having a place to find all this information helps us tremendously in educating us to do the right thing.

Initiative No. 2: Training and development

This initiative is probably the most important one, as continuous learning should be mandatory. The world around us is constantly changing, not just from a technological point of view, but in the way we do things, how we need to behave, what essential life skills we need to apply, in order to adapt to these changes and to ensure that from a development point of view we remain at the top of our game and in sync with our executives.

Training for most organizations is a standard budgeted item, but often only those who are perceived to add dollars to the bottom line are afforded the opportunity of ongoing training and development, and the assistant, the person that manages the manager, gets left behind as an afterthought – yes, we have to fend for ourselves. But that is okay, because having an internal network will cover all our training and developmental needs, where we can be the main initiators.

Sharing information, exchanging ideas, and taking time out to help our peers in our organization to be a part of the bigger and more successful picture, is what the internal network offers. Here you can facilitate training and developmental initiatives that will make your executives sit back and say "wow".

Let's have a further look at the initiatives we can host in-house for our peers that will add value and save money.

- **Portfolio of evidence assignments**, collated through various in-house sessions covering topics like communication, ethics, organizational skills, time management, minute taking, and conflict management. You, as the assistants, can facilitate these workshops. Within your internal network you can identify those assistants who are best at a particular topic and let them run with it. The learning from these is invaluable and connects assistants from across the organization.

- **Certified designation assignments**; these are linked to various training organizations that provide globally recognized certifications, for example the Advanced Certificate for the Executive Personal Assistant known as ACEPA (www.executivesecretary.com), and the IAAP, International Association of Administrative Professionals (www.iaap-hq.org). Having a certified designation as part of your personal development is invaluable, as it shows your current and any future employer that you take your profession very seriously, and have applied a learner-for-life attitude in ensuring that your skills are constantly updated in line with the CPD (Continued Professional Development) that goes with the certification. This means that once you have completed the program, in order to retain your certification you need to ensure you earn points (CPD points) within a certain time frame. You earn these points by attending certified training courses approved by various certified vendors.

For me, personally, one of the best initiatives ever implemented at my organization's internal network was that of **Induction Training**, which was aimed at any new assistants entering the organization, as well as assistants who needed refresher courses, those who had moved departments and now needed to learn how to do a new process, and those assistants who wanted to teach operational processes to the above.

- **Induction Training** can be a huge hit, and is vital in helping the new assistant get started with everything they need to support their manager and their teams almost immediately they start their job. It is always a very daunting and scary feeling for any new person joining an organization. How do we book meeting rooms, order stationery, and who do we use to arrange travel arrangements, pay invoices and source products? The internal assistant network covers all these issues for the assistant in one easily accessible folder, and at the same time, without the managers even realizing it, gives the assistant the head start they need to be productive almost immediately they hit their seat!

- **Training providers**; of course we need to know who the best companies are to go to for external training, and what are the essential Summits and Conferences assistants should be attending to gain expertise knowledge, to network and to grow their professions. In this part of your intranet, you should have a folder listing all the certified training providers. To help you get started here are my top suggestions: Executive Secretary Live events (www.executivesecretarylive. com), Be The Ultimate Assistant workshops with Bonnie Low-Kramen (www.bonnielowkramen.com), Vickie Sokol-Evans and everything Microsoft (www. redcapeco.com), Julie Perrine and All Things Admin (www.allthingsadmin.com). There are tons more, but these should help get you going.

- **Belonging to Networks**: There are a lot of assistant networks and associations out there. Executive Secretary has a full list of all registered associations on the back page of all their magazine publications. I highly recommend that you familiarize yourself first with each network's offerings before deciding to join. Investigate who they offer membership to (is it for all and sundry under the "administrative" umbrella, or is it for the secretarial profession?) and who actually runs these associations – are they run and managed by people who run their own business interests alongside the association, are they dedicated assistants with full-time jobs, or have they quit their executive assistant job to run a network? Be aware of what and who you are selecting. Although many do offer a varied range of resources, I prefer to stick with what will be good for me as an executive assistant and enhance my knowledge and skills. I prefer a network that is run by assistants for assistants, and that their primary focus is our profession. Be aware that different countries refer to the executive assistant differently. In South Africa 'admins' are those people who do clerical-related duties, whereas in the USA 'admins' are in fact executive assistants and management assistants and so on, who support managers and their teams. My favourite networks are www.platinumassist.org.za , followed by www.epaa.org. uk.

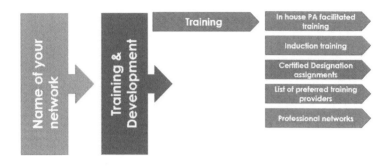

Initiative No. 3: Networking events

The power of networking should never be underestimated. The value it brings back to our offices is immense. I rather like the analogy of "charity starts at home", where the assistant should network and understand their own organization first, and I will give you some ideas further down the line.

Then of course there has to be networking outside of the organization for the assistant. We are the ones who manage our managers, and are always on the lookout for opportunities to learn more from our competitors, potential clients and future partnerships. We are also keen to source different suppliers and, probably more importantly, to share experiences and exchange solutions to the challenges that are common to all assistants. We need our circle of peers.

There is a story I can share with you, where not so long ago my executive had been having endless problems and service issues with his internet provider. He himself had been sitting on the phone for many hours, hoping for someone to help him with his problem. He normally closes his door when he attends to his personal issues, but on this particular day I overheard his frustration and annoyance.

After hearing him slamming down the phone, I went into his office and asked him for all the particulars of his query. Within less than an hour his long-standing complaint was resolved. There was no secret to this fix. It was simple. Through networking with my peers I met and knew the CEO's assistant from that internet provider. Need I say more? And there have been many other situations in which through my network I was able to save my executive from himself!

Let's now turn our focus on those networking events which you can include as part of this initiative:

- Attendance of Assistant Summits and major conferences,

- Attending or hosting Vendor EXPO's,

- Celebrating National Administrative Day or Secretaries Day (depending on which country you live in),

- Annual Assistant Awards events, either in-house or external,

- Celebrating National Boss's Day,

- Organizing your own in-house Assistants Conference (numbers-dependent),

- Organizational product sessions (learn what your company actually does),

- Community initiatives,

- Network educational,

- Lunch hour visits by inspirational and motivational speakers and award-winning assistants.

A great suggestion for your own internal network is to provide your peers with an opportunity to learn more about the other departments' functions and operations within your organization. These can be hosted by the assistant who knows the most about a particular department. Another suggestion is to invite your procurement department to give updates of new processes being implemented, or provide a session where the assistant has the opportunity to give input into an existing process which may not be working well, and where there could be lots of problems and issues. Engaging with the right people and sorting out operational problems in a friendly forum is such a great idea. Problems are resolved and issues can be ironed out.

It is also a good idea to create an events calendar which can be accessed and viewed by your peer community. One rule we do need to reiterate though is that the internal assistant network should always add value to our jobs and our organizations, and that all initiatives are work related.

One of the most profound lessons I learnt from being part of an internal network was that it doesn't matter who you work for, your ideas and suggestions have value, there are no stupid questions, and combined as a committee serving your peer community, you also get the opportunity to better understand your peers and learn to respect them for who they are and the contributions they make. One person's idea is of great value, but the ideas of many will have phenomenal results.

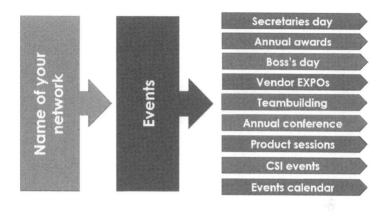

Initiative No 4: Resources

Resources are an essential part of any internal network toolkit. Assistants want to know where to go to for visa information, which restaurants are the best, who they should use for team builds, what florists supply the best value for money, where to find the best deal for your organization's branded merchandise, where you can go on the organization's intranet to find templates, which apps will work best for them and their managers, and everything in-between. Ideally this folder will be accessible from your organization's intranet, and will include links accompanied by a brief overview of the product or service, enabling the assistant to go directly to the approved service or product. Yes, Google is our friend, but it doesn't always give us an immediate or best result.

Having resources readily available on our intranet provides quick links and access to those tools which will help us in our daily lives.

There is an additional resource that, although it is not necessarily one that needs to be on the intranet, is one that provides almost instantaneous assistance. At my organization we have what we call an "Ask PACE" WhatsApp group. PACE, by the way, stands for PA Centre of Excellence. How this WhatsApp group works is simple; we added all the mobile numbers of the assistants into the group, and every time someone needs help or direction, they message their request to the group and within seconds they get a response.

This resource is by far one of our best yet. The example on this page is a real-time snapshot of how quick the response for help is. I highly recommend it.

Under the Map Links intranet tab (see the diagram on the next page), it's a great idea to provide the GPS coordinates as well as the full address and a picture of a map. With Google maps available on most mobile phones, you can save directions on your manager's mobile quickly and easily. Yes, I know that many of them have GPS in their cars, but you and I know that some of our managers are technologically challenged. Best to be prepared!

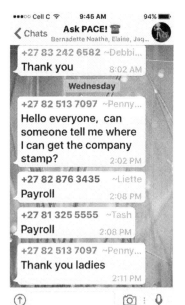

Providing templates of itineraries which get circulated is a great idea and a nice template to include in your toolkit of resources; however we also need to be aware that the itinerary can be created directly from your managers' diary (in Outlook for example).

One resource I have not included in the diagram below is the handover document. A template of this should be made available for all assistants, especially for those who may be away for extended periods of time, for those of us who leave the organization, and for when we go on vacation and someone else needs to help out.

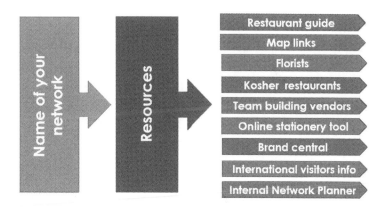

Initiative No. 5: Assistant Hub

This is the last of the suggested initiatives for your intranet site, the Assistant Hub, or you could potentially call it the PA Forum, whichever fits your culture and your organization. This initiative section is where you can find all the information related to your profession, your network, short tips, advice and a little bit of sanity.

Here is the right place to **showcase your workgroup**, the peers behind the initiatives and the processes, the legacy makers old and new. Your assistant community wants to know who runs the internal network, what we look like and who we are. So a good idea here is to provide a great colour photograph of each member of the internal network, together with a brief biography about each member; who they work for, how long they have been in the organization, their achievements, their future dreams and what makes them the awesome assistants that they are.

On our intranet site we provide **links** to external resources and training like Executive Secretary Magazine and its live events, Be The Ultimate Assistant workshops and books by Bonnie Low-Kramen, Vickie Sokol-Evans, Melba Duncan, Anel Martin Training, ACEPA training, all Julie Perrine's 'how to's, etc. Our community loves this section and, of course, we send out email snippets of anything new that comes in, and share it with our assistant community.

Birthdays need to be celebrated, and here we share a list of birthdates, which is updated on a regular basis, so that we can celebrate this special time with our peers. What is great about having a birthday list is that you can also set it up to send you a reminder in your calendar and then post your personalized birthday wish for your friend on the WhatsApp group for your internal network. I cannot tell you what awesome goodwill this small act of kindness breeds. It is just amazing and brings us closer as a team.

There are always superstars among us, and we need to showcase and celebrate each other's greatness. I am a strong believer in raising up my peers, celebrating their achievements and making sure they are recognized. Having a "**Wall of Fame**" is fantastic. It inspires others to reach the same heights and encourages our peers to also want to achieve. We have National Assistant winners and finalists past and present in our organization, those who have won internal organizational awards, those who have created opportunities, participated in community projects, contributed to our profession and have enhanced the lives and wellbeing of those around them. Celebrate each other – raise each other up. Announce it!

The **knowledge update** section provides our internal network an opportunity to attend short, one hour sessions updating us on our organization's products or processes. These are normally hosted as and when the need arises, to showcase new initiatives like a new travelling tool or a new product being introduced by our organization. We need to ensure that we are always up to date on what our organization does, what our products or services are, and when there are changes in either of these. We also get the expert involved with that particular product or process to address our internal network members.

There are those among us that are **specialists** at specific skills. We need to be able to collaborate with them when we do various projects for our managers. Some of these expert assistants among us are Excel Experts, PowerPoint Professors and MS Word Masters. We need to know who they are, where they reside in our organization and how we can contact them quickly. We also need to know who the Travel Tipsters, the Budget Beavers and Event Divas are too, so go ahead and create that Specialists folder – we all need it!

Having a dedicated **notice board** for our internal network gives us access to all the personal stuff we want to share, sell, exchange and advertise. Some organizations may already have one for staff, so try not to duplicate or reinvent the wheel. Make sure though that you first seek permission from your organization to have such an e-notice board.

The Assistant Hub folder can include anything that cannot otherwise be categorized, but which is still important and has a shared value amongst your assistant community. What I have listed is an example of what you can include. Use your imagination, but consider your organization's culture and values to ensure there is no conflict of interest, and avoid creating folders that can be replaced with an app or which already exist within your organization's intranet. We are here to make the space productive and useful.

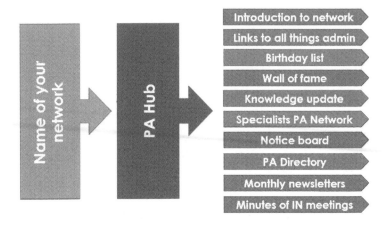

An internal assistant network will add a tremendous amount of value to all aspects of the assistant's role. Money is saved on training as this is now a shared value support network facilitated by the experts amongst you. We become more productive because we are saving time by having quick and effective access to resources, and one of our most important initiatives is that of creating and maintaining standards right across the board, ensuring our organization's reputation is aligned to a good work ethic, a great brand, and teamwork. Everyone is on the same page and working together collectively as a team.

An assistant network offers the opportunity for the assistant to become a superstar in their role because they are constantly informed by it and actively participate in its success.

3

Ready, Set, Go!

In Chapter 2 I gave you the "Why". In this chapter I am going to cover the "How". It is all very well having all these fantastic ideas and initiatives, but how are we going to manage and maintain them? Where do we start and who gets involved?

Right from the get-go I have to be honest with you and say: it isn't going to be easy. You will always have a group of assistants who don't want to participate because they are too "busy", those who may not "like" what is on offer, assistants who come forward with more reasons why not to have one, and those that are just plain jealous that you thought of the idea in the first place. There will be egos to work around and all sorts of other low-EQ attributes which may make you a tad seasick. (EQ here means Emotional Quotient like IQ means Intelligence Quotient.)

But please, don't let them stop you from reaching your goal – as you progress with the initiative, keep a cool head and don't get offended by the nay-sayers. You will succeed, I can assure you and, most importantly, you will win most of them over by the time you host your first event!

Step 1: Gathering the troops for boot camp

We are now at the point where you need to start pulling the troops in, and by the troops I am referring to those assistants with whom you have shared your vision, your dream to make life for the assistant a much more pleasurable experience. We have discussed what an internal network is, we have dissected it piece by piece, and we realize that there are many components to it, so we know that LOTS of work needs to be done or committed to before we can go further.

At this point I highly recommend that you and your handful of faithful troops all get together to strategize and plan the way ahead. For you it is going to be relatively easy as I have already mapped out your route, you just need to decide on a couple of things, work through the steps that follow and be able to pull it all together at the end. But first, you definitely need to host a strategy session.

Plan a strategy day, out of the office with your new committee. You can either host the strategy session offsite from your offices by asking for a site visit at one of the local hotel venues, where you are likely to get the use of their facilities and a lunch for free, or you can have your strategy session at the office. I prefer hosting the strategy sessions offsite, as there are fewer interruptions and it also gives everyone an opportunity to get to know each other on a more personal level. Your session should be for a minimum of one day. When we plan ours, we normally have them as a site visit at an out of town venue where we get to sleep out for one night. We spend the evening getting to know each other and participate in "get to know" games.

At the morning-after breakfast, which is generally also free, we gather in a meeting room to plan and map out our vision for our network. Make sure to bring along some flip chart paper, at least one laptop, and as the initiator it is a good idea to draw up an agenda, either one based on the topics from this book, or one specific to your organization.

In Chapter 7, I have included an actual workbook for you, which you can photocopy and bring along for each member attending. It's a fantastic resource to guide you along your way.

Here then is your suggested bootcamp agenda:

1   Set out your objectives,

2   From your objectives choose a few realistic things you would like to achieve within your internal assistant network for the next year,

3   Allocate responsibilities that are required to accomplish your objectives,

4   Draw up a budget,

5   Draw up a calendar of events with timelines,

6   Present your proposal to management,

7   And most importantly, have fun!

Step 2: Managing expectations

On the upside, being the initiator and legacy maker of a project of this magnitude teaches you so many valuable lessons. When I started with our Assistant Forum 16 years ago, it was a bit of a circus to begin with. Everyone had an opinion, and those who didn't were never heard, but what transpired as time went on is that you develop leadership skills, because you have to make sure that everyone is involved and everyone has the opportunity to share their story and opinions. From the early days I realized the importance of EQ in a group, consisting mainly of women, and having to deal with all the bitching on the sidelines. You have to nip it in the bud and make sure there is no gossiping behind each other's backs – it just breeds contempt and distrust, and you don't want that in your committee!

Just for a quick reality check, here is a short list of what to expect.

At first, not every assistant in your organization will want to participate. Accept this. You don't need to have every assistant on board, and neither should you force them. Once the assistants realize what they are missing out on, they will come and join you. The more informative and value-added your network, the more participation you will attract.

If you are an executive assistant or the EA to the CEO or Chairman, you will get resistance from the middle management band of assistants if you come over too strong and autocratic. The secret here is to not throw your weight around or to display any form of arrogance based on your title or position. What you need to do if you are the most senior assistant initiating the network, is to be humble and respectful, and ensure that you include even the most junior of assistants in your start up. And always remember: if you want respect, you give respect, no matter the age between participants.

If you are not the most senior assistant in the organization, remember that you don't necessarily need that assistant's approval. What I do encourage is that you invite that assistant, together with your other selected assistants, to your initial meeting where your ideas for an internal network will be shared. Take into consideration that you will also have to deal with some negativity, but stay strong and be resilient to your cause. And again, humility and open-mindedness are key.

Then there are the managers, whose first impression will be that it is a club of some sort. You will need to be absolutely thorough in your proposal preparation to make sure that they see the value and cost savings involved in a network. There will, however, be some managers that may need more convincing than others, and the best way around this is to assure them that they will be playing an active role in some of the initiatives to ensure they get a return on investment (ROI). Again, stand your ground. Remember that anything that is worth something is worth fighting for.

Be aware that you may have to start your network without any funds from your organization, but that is fine, as a shared load is always made lighter, and as assistants we will work with the resources we have. And besides, you don't really need a budget to start off with, but as your network initiatives and outputs grow, your managers will see the value and a budget can be established.

Last but not least, you (or your elected chairperson) will have to make it very clear right from the start that those who have voluntarily offered to participate in your workgroup or committee are in it for the long haul. Your network is not a forum to provide them with a glamorous title, or any forms of entitlement or special treatment. Setting up, managing and maintaining an internal network takes hard work, commitment and dedication. Being a committee member is not for lazy people.

Step 3: Not a one man show

As you have by now realized, you simply cannot do this on your own. You will need to gather the troops and invite those assistants with whom you have shared your vision with thorough discussions, to help you get started. It is always a good idea to have a few like-minded assistants on your side (taking into consideration those suggestions as mentioned above, and depending on where you are positioned on the company pecking order), and once the decision amongst yourselves has been made, the idea now needs to become an action plan and then a reality.

Step 4: Deciding on your audience

This all depends on you and your committee. You may wish to just include all the executive, management and personal assistants, or extend it to all admins and receptionists. My organization's internal network is just for assistants; those of us who fall into the secretarial support function. Our roles are uniquely management partnerships and not admins.

My suggestion is to start off with only assistants, and then as you progress and get better at managing and maintaining your network, you can invite other support staff. But this is entirely up to you and your team. Keeping it to just assistants is more realistic for me, but you will need to consider your organizational structure, culture and ethos. Be mindful of these things. The last thing you need to do is to step on someone's toes or come across as offensive.

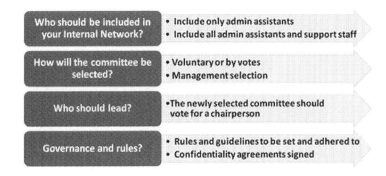

Who should be included in your Internal Network?	• Include only admin assistants • Include all admin assistants and support staff
How will the committee be selected?	• Voluntary or by votes • Management selection
Who should lead?	• The newly selected committee should vote for a chairperson
Governance and rules?	• Rules and guidelines to be set and adhered to • Confidentiality agreements signed

You and your new team will be regarded as game changers, role players and legacy makers. You will be embarking on a project that will forever mention your names in the history books as the forerunners, the ones who were not afraid to take on the challenge of innovation and initiate your organization's first ever internal network. So, are you ready?

No teams are successful without preparation, rules and the allocation and accountability of responsibilities, and remember that "teamwork makes the dream work".

Step 5: Roles and responsibilities

Each member of your team should be allocated an area of responsibility. Ask what each member would like to be responsible for, or be the team leader for. People are likely to choose tasks which they believe they have a skill set for, are comfortable with, or they believe they can learn something new from. Be open to their contribution of participation and responsibility, and as the leader of the pack, ensure that you encourage the experts among you to take up roles on your committee as well, to ensure that each team is well balanced with a mix of experts, people at intermediary level, and learners amongst them. It is an empowering experience to be part of such an initiative; make sure you are the one empowering others.

Try to encourage assistants from the different departments within the organization to take on roles similar to the department in which they currently work. For example, if you intend having a budget for your network, you will need to appoint a treasurer to control the internal network's budget and finances, so opt for the services of the assistant who works in or for the financial and accounts department. They will have inside knowledge, and may be more able to contribute in terms of skill and value in the area of finances than others. But don't let this limit you. Your committee will work well if all those on it are active contributors, irrespective of which department they work in.

Step 6: Structuring your committee

It is important that your committee is formed on mutual respect, trust and commitment. You simply cannot go into this initiative believing that one person is more important than another. A committee is just really a fancy name for a team – no matter how you look at it, you are all a team, and all in it together. If one fails the committee fails, and always remember you are only as strong as the weakest person on your team. So be prepared to reach out to each other, raise each other up, motivate and encourage each other.

I cannot express enough what a fantastic leadership and EQ learning experience this initiative is. When you are part of an internal network you will come across many personalities and will have to deal with many levels of emotions. It is the ideal learning ground for gaining important leadership skills. You need to be honest without being mean, and to be open to everyone's ideas and suggestions, even if you think the idea is lousy. Allow everyone an opportunity to express themselves. You will be able to tell who the quieter ones are amongst you; address them gently for their input. Inclusion is key.

Ideally you would need to find assistants who would be best suited to fill the following roles:

- Chairperson

- Treasurer

- Secretary

- Initiatives team members

Let's look at each of these roles in more detail.

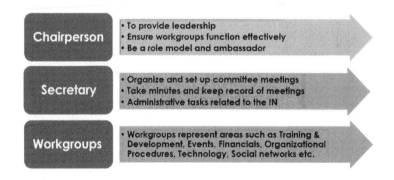

Chairperson

There are two ways in which you can elect a chairperson. The first one is by votes obtained from within your committee, and the second by votes from your assistant community. A chairperson should not be self-elected. Your network ethics should be based on honesty, trust and democracy. It is, after all, a team effort. The repercussions of voting yourself in as a chairperson will be far reaching, as it will only create dissent and resentment. The role of chairperson should also not be given to someone who is the most senior or longest serving in the organization. If your chairperson is selected fairly, the chances of succeeding are multiplied.

The next thing to consider is how long a chairperson should hold office for. I recommend that a year is a good term for office. Thereafter, you can elect someone else as chairperson. By rotating leadership it provides the opportunity for other assistants to apply leadership skills. You will all be there to guide the chairperson and provide support. The rule here should be that only members of the workgroup who would like to be up for nomination of the role should be included. It will be pointless voting in an assistant who doesn't actually want the role.

In order to ensure that the role of chairperson is appropriately appointed, it is recommended that the process be kept simple and democratic, but also fair and professional. The ideal process to follow would be:

- Set up a date and time to host the voting process and seek the assistance of an independent staff member or Human Resources representative.

- Create a list of names of assistants who are keen to be nominated as chairperson, and create a voting form with a brief resume on each of the nominees. Place a block on the right hand side of the form where committee members can make a cross next to the candidate of their choice.

- Once completed, the voting form must be forwarded to the independent staff member or Human Resources representative, who will then count the votes and advise the committee on completion.

- If a tie occurs, a re-vote must take place with only the tied candidates' names being considered for the position.

(Note that there are also a number of free election systems available online that could be used instead of paper, e.g. electionrunner.com.)

A short list of criteria can be minuted and kept on file for future reference.

The role of the chairperson is not to make independent decisions when there is an impasse on a decision that needs to be made. The chairperson is someone who shows leadership skills, who can motivate, inspire and encourage the workgroup, but also ensure that project commitments are met and agreed goals reached.

Treasurer

The role of treasurer is determined by whether or not you will be managing a budget. It should be taken on by an assistant who knows something about finances and accounting, and, as mentioned above, someone who might already support a financial department. The role of treasurer is voluntary, and if there are two or more assistants applying for this role, a vote should take place within the workgroup to determine who gets it. Both candidates for the role must be excluded from voting.

The role of the treasurer is to draw up a cost-effective and prudent budget for the internal network, to manage the expenses that occur within the network, and to ensure that the same policies that apply to the governance of the organization's funds apply to the network budget. The Treasurer may not necessarily be the one authorizing expenses, this could be a cost centre manager, or someone within the organization who has the authority to do so. This is a discussion you will need to have to ensure that the right process is followed.

If you are fortunate enough to be granted a network budget, never ever abuse it. Misappropriation of company funds will lead to disciplinary action or even dismissal. Make sure that you use the funds in the same manner as your own hard earned money. Just because a budget has been approved for your network does not mean you have money to treat your audience to spa treatments and unnecessary gifts.

Secretary

I always have a good giggle when it comes to filling this role, as we are all "secretaries", and many of us already do the minutes, send out meeting agendas and set up meetings, but when you ask the group who would like the role, funnily enough it takes a while before you find a volunteer – and here I thought we love being assistants!

You will need a dedicated Secretary who will take minutes and notes, send out meeting agendas and manage the secretarial duties for your workgroup. Whoever takes on this role must be prepared to put in the effort and commit 100% to ensuring meetings and minutes are managed properly. You don't want someone who takes the minutes, but then keeps the committee waiting weeks to view them.

Initiatives team members

This is where the fun really begins! Just so that we are all on the same page, I want to mention that those assistants who will be fulfilling the above mentioned roles can and should also be part of the initiatives teams – remember TEAM – we all work together!

For every initiative you decide you want your internal network to have, you need a team leader and one or two co-conspirators. Some initiatives may only need one person, but something like, for example, running an induction program for assistants will require that all hands are on deck. Likewise if you decide to host a conference, your entire team would need to participate.

Step 7: Ensuring corporate governance

It is essential that once your committee is officially formed there are rules set, a confidentiality agreement signed by all participants, as well as a Code of Conduct and associated actions which will be taken should the rules not be adhered to. An internal network committee will be privy to confidential and sensitive information, and it is therefore important to set boundaries for your committee, and ensure the right compliance framework is in place.

One of the main reasons we have all the committee members sign a confidentiality agreement is that there are often times when managers may approach the team to mentor or coach their PAs, and certain information shared regarding another assistant should remain confidential.

We have now worked through most of the detail, but in order to bring this all together we need to ensure that the operational side of our new internal network is taken care of and the administration functions and the role of each of the committee members are effectively managed.

4

Working on a Budget

It is important, but not essential at first, to have a budget from which to work. Most organizations do set aside a budget facility for training purposes for their employees. It is a good idea to establish what this budget is and to suggest that the costs budgeted for the assistants be transferred into a separate internal assistant network's expense centre. By doing this, a budget will be automatically created without disrupting the base expenses of the organization. What we are doing is transferring the budgeted training costs of each assistant into a separate expense account and naming it 'Internal Network'.

Establishing an approved budget for the internal network is highly advantageous for the organization, as it provides a clearer view of how the training costs for assistants is being allocated. Often in large organizations some assistants get to go on many training initiatives and can overspend their training budgets, while other assistants are constantly being told there is no budget for them. Establishing an approved budget creates transparent and fair visibility to ensure that all assistants have the same opportunities to attend training – the difference being, though, that you will be facilitating your own in-house educational initiatives, run by the experts within your organization, the knowledgeable and skilful assistants.

This is exactly how we run our internal network at Discovery where either I or other assistants facilitate full-day workshops at no cost for ourselves or to the organization. To give you an idea of the savings involved, I have facilitated well over 16 training initiatives over the last five years alone. If I were to equate the average cost of one full day workshop at approximately R7000 (which is about the average rate), multiply that by the number of assistants in my organization (an average over the last five years of 110 assistants) attending a one day workshop, that equates to R112 000. Now multiply that figure of R112 000 by 16 events = R1 792 000.00. To be honest, I didn't even realize this value until I calculated it for this example – and this is just the training end of the internal network.

What should we be budgeting for?

Bear in mind that your internal network budget should not be seen as an additional expense to your organization; in fact the internal network is that much of a value-add that it saves money through its many resources and cost–saving initiatives.

So what kind of potential expenses do we need to take into consideration in preparing our budget? Here is a sample list of the most important ones that come to mind:

✓ Training and development

✓ External seminars and conferences

✓ Assistant Network annual conference

- ✓ Travel costs for out of town assistants

- ✓ Gifts for invited special guests and visitors

- ✓ Secretaries Day or Administrative Assistant Day

- ✓ National Boss's Day

- ✓ Internal network strategy sessions (and here you can save money by getting by on a "site-visit" pass at various venues)

- ✓ Stationery and printing

- ✓ Books related to our industry which educate

- ✓ Professional and network memberships

- ✓ Catering for workshop and annual conference events

- ✓ Rewards and recognition initiatives

- ✓ Subscription fees to assistant-related magazines like Executive Secretary Magazine

How do we formulate our budget?

- ✓ Work on a per-head basis (per assistant)

- ✓ Obtain quotes through research to find values as close as possible to the real cost of the expense

- ✓ Type it all up into an Excel spreadsheet, and make sure your calculations are 100% correct

✓ Meet with your financial manager or finance director and ask for their input and guidance

The following is an example of how we structured our budget for our internal network. Feel free to adjust it according to your own requirements, using the same formula, or as guided by your finance manager.

DESCRIPTION	No.	COST PER HEAD	BUDGET	EXPLANATION
PA Centre Of Excellence				
Proposed Budget For 2016				
June 2015 PA Headcount = 110		110		Headcount increased from 98 to 116 (12)
Previous Cost Centre No: D187				
TRAINING AND DEVELOPMENT				
Bespoke training workshops	4	R 1,500.00	R 165,000.00	Discovery PA Masterclass Series (4 modules proposed for 2015)
Business information sessions for PAs	6	R 100.00	R 66,000.00	To be hosted in-house every second month (6 times a year)
Discovery PACE Annual Conference	1	R 1,000.00	R 110,000.00	To be hosted externally, annually on Secretaries Day
STRATEGY SESSIONS				
Focus Group strategy sessions	2	R 1,000.00	R 24,000.00	Only for Focus Group members (approximately 12 PAs)

OTHER				
External training (NCBA)	10	R 12,000.00	R 120,000.00	Will be dependent on how many PAs take the opportunity.
Subscription to Professional Association	1	R 230.00	R 25,300.00	
Stationery and printing			R 18,000.00	Cost of printing training manuals, invitations and other stationery
Travel costs	8	R 3,500.00	R 28,000.00	For Discovery PAs
Accommodation cost	8	R 1,000.00	R 8,000.00	For Discovery PAs
Transport cost	8	R 500.00	R 4,000.00	For Discovery PAs
Car / bus rental	4	R 4,500.00	R 18,000.00	External events like off-site visits and teambuilding events 4x a year
Staff entertainment and gifts			R 10,000.00	For external visitors and thank you gifts
Courier service			R 2,000.00	Documents to be sent via courier to regional PAs
Team building event	1	R 650.00	R 63,700.00	To be hosted once a year
Professional fees			R 40,000.00	For the use of invited speakers and facilitators
TOTAL BUDGET	Total cost per PA = R6381		R 702,000.00	

5

Marketing, Mailers, Desk Drops And Launching

We have now established a basic foundation for the core reasons for having an internal network within your organization, but how do we sell this idea, how do we get buy-in from not only our managers but also the other assistants in our organization to participate? How you market your idea, and the fantastic initiatives behind this project, is up to you and your team. However, I have some suggestions below which you may want to consider, ideas that have worked for my particular internal network at my organization.

Here are four essential tips to marketing your internal network:

1 **Be available:** You and your workgroup are primarily here for your peer community. You need to ensure you are available to help them access resources, assist them with information and give them the opportunity to empower themselves by encouraging them to attend your training and in-house events.

2 **Respond positively to requests:** Your managers and your peers will be watching you and will expect you and your team to deliver purposefully and with intent. Your responses to questions and help need to be quick. Our internal network created the WhatsApp group which I have spoken about earlier in this book. This is a fantastic way to respond quickly and efficiently to your peer group requests.

3 **Collaborate with your peers:** You need to be open to their suggestions and feedback. You need to be aware of their needs, which may become your needs too. We learn from each other when we collaborate with each other.

4 **Add the personal touch:** Be genuine in your interactions, remember to send flowers, cards or gifts when there is a reason to celebrate. Congratulate your peers on jobs well done.

From hosting your strategy session you will have already discovered that you need a list of all the assistants in your organization (and possibly also the receptionists and other admins). You must make sure your list is continually updated. Your assistant list should not just have the person's name listed but also their department, who they work for, perhaps also their birthdate as well. Having an internal network is mainly for work purposes, but we do need some balance and celebrating birthdays is one of the special touches we can add to our network.

You need to ensure that any new assistants who join your organization also get included on your list for future communications, so make sure you collaborate with the right Human Resources people who can alert you when this happens. Ideally this would be the assistant from Human Resources.

So we have our list of names all sorted, now we need to create an email distribution group. Once this is finalized we can start sending out emails to invite our peers to participate in internal network initiatives and events. Some of the kinds of emails you will be sending are:

- **Alerts** of new processes to follow with directions to your Intranet files where they can be located.

- **Notifications** of departmental out-of-office alerts. These notifications come in very handy if you are planning to order forex, and an alert comes out to say the Treasury department will be out of the office on Friday – you then have enough time to arrange forex before that.

- **Information** emails can be related to training events, birthday announcements etc.

Make sure your emails are clear and concise and that you have double-checked your grammar and spelling. You should also, if you can, get your graphic designers to design funky email banners for your internal network – these add a touch of class and professionalism to your email and distinctly brand your network.

Once all the elements of your assistant network have been consolidated (roles and responsibilities, budget, network initiatives), arrange a meeting with the management team, or your Human Resources Director and, as a committee, present your proposal to them. A proposal template is given in Chapter 7.

Your proposal also needs to be clear and concise. You will be presenting it to your executive team, and it is likely that you will be allocated five minutes to put forward your proposal. You need to make sure that you have put the right effort, research, planning and consideration into it. Here are some essential steps to follow.

Do your research: the first thing you must take into consideration is that you want to show your executive team that you understand your organization's culture, and the challenges your assistants face. Gather as much data as you can about your assistant community, like numbers, geographical locations, which managers they work for and if they work for more than one. Keep your professional hat on to ensure you think like an executive and you don't get carried away with trivial or emotional pieces of research that will be meaningless to a highly motivated executive team.

Think of the long term: It is all good and well to have a great idea, but if you are not able to maintain it once you have implemented it, it may come to naught. You and your team need to think on a strategic level about how you are going to maintain your internal network and give it the longevity it deserves. Make sure that the solutions you give are sustainable and achievable. Providing management with your vision and mission will be a positive indication that you and your group have given the initiative all the thought it deserves, and this is likely to establish a feeling of trust between yourselves, your group of peers and your executives.

Don't rush into it: Yes, I understand that you are keen to get going on your projects, and you may have already decided on when you want certain stages of your initiatives completed by. It is important, however, to take the time to ensure that you have included realistic timelines, reasonable budget figures, and that every "t" is crossed and "i" dotted.

And last but not least, **ensure your proposal contains facts**. Your executives will question the validity of some of your statements, probably only because they have never really been given the data that you are providing them with, so they can hardly believe the cost savings that an internal network offers.

How you present your proposal is entirely up to you. I recommend that you do it in a documented form, with your new internal network branding, as well as a 4-page PowerPoint presentation slide. I recommend that at least two members of your team be part of the delegation to take it to your executive team. The presenter does not have to be your chairperson; however I would choose someone from your team who is not shy, who understands your internal network ambitions, and who can easily answer questions and present confidently.

It is VITAL that you have the buy-in of the managers, because without it, it will be extremely difficult to run and maintain an internal network. In this presentation you will need to present your objectives (what you would like to achieve and what value it is going to add), as well as to note all the initiatives you and the workgroup will be undertaking. You also need to include an overview of your budget (explained in an earlier chapter with a budget template available in the same chapter).

Once you have approached management and they are happy with the proposal and accept it – and if co-ordinated and well-thought-through it will definitely get their buy-in – set up a time to do a launch to the rest of the assistant community.

Before you announce the approval of the network to your assistant community, it would be great to do desk drops, with an encrypted message that will get them wondering what's up. It will give a sense of excitement and anticipation. Think of novel ways you can make them excited.

On the day of your launch, if you do decide to have one, make sure you plan well in advance, send meeting invitations that get accepted and saved in the individual's calendar, so there can be no excuses that nobody knew about it. Make sure you also try and arrange some lucky prize draws and giveaways where possible.

When you do your presentation make it compelling and exciting, and if you need help – shout! I am only an email away, Cathyh@disovery.co.za. Give them an overview of your strategy for the year ahead and the activities you have planned. Remember to keep them informed, and use any feedback from them as constructive. Don't be offended, and don't take negative feedback personally, it is, after all, their assistant network, you and your team are the ambassadors.

6

Case Studies

Case study 1

The empowered admin network at Janssen Pharmaceutica Belgium

by Danielle de Wulf

At Janssen Pharmaceutica, a company of Johnson & Johnson, the admin network is a real WIN-WIN for all: the admins craft their job towards 2025 while management receives higher value support! (Let's agree on the terminology used: admins include all levels of secretaries and assistants, management, personal, executive, virtual... Managers include all bosses, supervisors, leaders, directors, Vice Presidents, CEOs etc). Danielle, one of the 230 management assistants who support 5000 colleagues in different sites in Belgium and the Netherlands, is proud to present their network model.

How did we build our network?

Our story started in 2010, when some of us felt dissatisfied for various reasons. Depending on our manager, we had too much or not enough work, experienced more or less flexibility to attend trainings and international meetings or to work from home occasionally. Holidays were less enjoyable because we were worrying about the amount of workload when returning to our desks, and sometimes we missed career opportunities because we were informed too late or were unaware of the vacancy.

Therefore we decided to join forces and created a network community with approximately 30 admins. We started by sharing info, tips, and best practices, and, later on, also workload. The other 200 admins gradually realized that they were missing out on updates, opportunities and vacancies, so we expanded. Since 2015 we can proudly announce that all 230 admins in Belgium and the Netherlands are part of one of our 15 teams. Our smallest team counts eight admins, the largest one 35 colleagues. Sometimes a team comprises all admins on one location or from the same department, sometimes it is cross-departmental, whatever works best.

For each team, we appointed **team leads**: volunteers wanting to explore their leadership skills in a safe environment. These 'captains' now meet monthly to discuss what's new and solve workload issues.

Extra flex pools support our teamwork

We have an internal flex team of seven admins with a permanent contract, but their mission is to solve temporary needs. We call them "flying doctors" because they go and help where there is an issue, like a peak in workload or because a colleague is on pregnancy or sick leave.

These flying ladies are very experienced and extremely flexible, they adore change and adapt quickly. Since they help in many different departments, they pick up best practices and have the mandate to propose efficiency enhancements. They are very welcome because they bring "a fresh pair of eyes" to the department and in return they receive more appreciation for their work.

We have a **pool of experts**, specialized in every procurement aspect, from ordering, contracting and paying to solving mismatches. These experts are a great blessing for all the admin colleagues who only occasionally need to make a purchase order, who would otherwise waste time finding out which procedures to follow. In 2017 we started another experiment, with a hub of admins doing travel and expense notes for different departments.

By clustering routine jobs that can be outsourced, admins can focus on the tasks where they can really make a difference. This lets us build an empowered network to become a future-proof, flexible, efficient and engaged self-steering community. Our **logo**, a puzzle piece fitting into the larger picture, reflects that we are part of the company and that admins support each other, uplifting their skills.

Sharing info in the network and building a communication SharePoint

Our different talents and interests are the strength of our network. We create opportunities to meet, share info and learn from each other. We also organize 'lunch & learn' sessions with inspirational speakers, sometimes external speakers but also any admin wishing to share knowledge or passion. So we all learn and grow.

To share our learnings, we created **MACS** (**M**anagement **A**ssistants **C**ommunication **S**ite), which is our own communication platform, where we post news, tips, updates, agenda for admin events and training, and growth opportunities. We communicate in a transparent way to all at the same time. The MACS archive gives people a way to retrieve information and this saves disc space.

Connecting internally and externally

By **connecting internally**, we help each other, resulting in quick wins and time savings. For example: we discovered it is more efficient to let one or two colleagues give a resume of procedural changes to their colleagues, rather than having each admin working her way through the entire manual. If several managers attend the same congress, it's more efficient to centralize travel bookings and registrations rather than have admins arranging the trip for their boss only.

We **connect externally** with schools that provide education to office management students, the admins of the future: we organize company tours and offer them traineeships. We give the event management students the opportunity to work out a real life event for us. Their teachers also join our training or speakers sessions, creating unique dynamics.

In return, the students' teachers keep us up-to-date on social media, presentation skills or other skills that were not part of our school training years ago.

How else do we inject new skills into our admins?

We take stock of our strengths and talents. We check what competencies our job will require towards 2025. We put together a **training plan** to close that gap and prepare all admins for the future.

These trainings range from technical skills to soft skills to project management and leadership skills. All our admins are encouraged to follow at least two trainings per year; they can choose one individually and the other one is mandatory with their team.

We developed a **Train the Admin Program**: new admins are trained and brought up to speed by an experienced colleague who is a certified trainer. This on the job training by their expert colleagues represents again huge time and energy savings for the hosting department. We changed our objective, from training only admins to training all functions, because management are increasingly expected to do admin work themselves, like booking travel.

How do we increase our employability and invest in our development?

Several development programs are available in our company but addressed to managers, therefore we re-created them for admins. In our **mentoring program**, the admin is coached by a director or someone at a higher level but the mentee is always in the driver's seat (e.g. use a mentor to learn how to give impactful presentations). In our **rotation project**, two admins swap departments temporarily or explore new horizons via an international experience. Or they can sign up to participate in **language lunches** to practice French, Spanish, German, English, and Italian.

What's in it for the admin?

- We are no longer working solo. We have an extensive network to help us.

- We save huge amounts of time because we can share best practices.

- There is transparency in opportunities and trainings.

- There are more growth and development possibilities and we are encouraged to make best use of our talents in our career path.

- This results in a better work-life balance and everyone has more fun and satisfaction in the job.

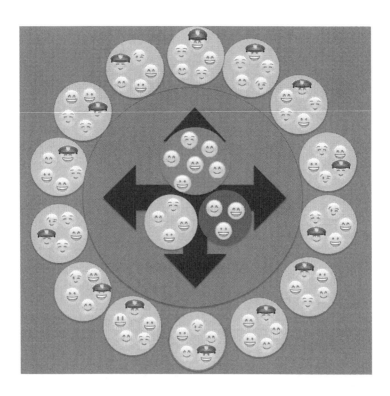

What does it require from the admin?

To foster this co-operation instinct, the **right mindset** is needed. We created an atmosphere of openness and trust, which avoids counterproductive job protection. It is safe to step out of our cocoon, it is rewarding to help each other and it is more efficient to communicate and share best practices and to avoid duplication of work.

What does our admin network model mean to management?

- We offer business continuity and flexibility.

- We propose innovative workload and process solutions.

- The wheel is not being reinvented, which results in considerable cost and efficiency savings.

- We have the strongest network and communication platform across departments and sites.

How do we offer workload solutions with our flex pools and guarantee business continuity?

The team lead or captain is the **Single Point of Contact** for the group, which makes it easy for managers when they have any issues related to workload. We have a **back-up** system for expected and unexpected absences, so business continuity is guaranteed. We make smart use of **idle time**. We dare to speak up, even about workload: if we have a dip because it is holiday season or our manager is on a business trip, we say so and help others out or take on a project. In return, we receive help when we have a peak in our workload.

We strive for a **fair workload and work pressure** for every admin, based on interests, talents, capabilities and ambitions. It's therefore crucial that the team lead and supervisor know what their admins want in order to match their interests with the business needs.

How do we simplify, streamline or improve processes?

There are about 35 different administrative systems at Janssen. As system experts we quickly notice inefficiencies. Suggestions for improvement are embraced. We assemble a team with expert admins, business partners and all the right stakeholders. Together, they try to find a solution that saves time, energy and money for all, and this solution is communicated via MACS, our dedicated admin website.

We tackle over a dozen processes, solving problems with travel or expense receipts and streamlining procedures company-wide. In fact, one third of our 230 admins are participating in one or more process groups on top of being part of a team. Indeed, lots of colleagues are thrilled to take ownership and more responsibility and to enlarge their circle of influence.

Eager to start your own internal network? Here are the ingredients:

Our robust framework is highly customizable because it's modular and reproducible in all kinds of settings and companies. Just pick what would work in your company.

1. Find believers

- You need **management and HR buy-in**.

- A **dedicated person** with an entrepreneurial spirit takes the lead of the admin team.

Quick adaptors will understand the benefits and more skeptical colleagues will follow as they realize that they miss a lot if they don't join. You will need time if you don't want to impose your model but let it grow bottom-up.

2. Ask for a budget

This money is to be spent on training and development.

3. Realize some quick wins

- Make a distribution list of all admins in your company. List your system experts.

- Get together in groups and learn from each other. You'll be amazed how you pick up things your colleagues do differently.

- Organize informal lunches with brainstorming on how to solve inefficiencies.

- Make sure all members inform their team lead about their strengths, talents, interests and ambitions so she can match the company's needs with the talents onboard.

- Show metrics to earn trust from your management. These metrics can be about budget, time and/or energy savings and "fewer frustrations".

Success!

Win for Assistants	Win for Management
Connect in extensive network	Workload solutions guarantee business continuity
Share info and best practices	Built-in flexibility with expert pools
Do jobcrafting based on talents & ambitions	Process optimisation
More transparancy in growth opportunities	Stimulation of cross departmental work
Fair workload Better work/life balance	Efficiency improvements generate cost savings

Danielle De Wulf holds a Bachelor degree in Office Management from Ghent, Belgium. She has 35 years of professional experience in different roles in pharmaceutical companies.

By supporting multiple global teams across various departments of Janssen (J&J), she has developed strong multilingual communication skills and built a large international network.

Over the last few years she has combined executive support with process and project lead roles: she has been engaged in the development of new business models for administrators and has been instrumental in their implementation and realization.

Danielle loves to share her inspiring story about 'how-to-network' with colleagues, school students and at cross-company forums. Contact her at ddwulf@its.jnj.com or via LinkedIn.

Case study 2

The Exeter PA Network

by Kim Glover of Michelmores

Exeter is a city in the region of Devon in the south west of England. The Exeter PA Network came about after Kim had attended an event hosted by another PA network in a neighbouring city (Plymouth) a few months previously. Kim was keen for Exeter to have something similar available to them and approached the organizer of the Plymouth Network, Christine Henshall-Hill, to seek her support in launching the Exeter Network.

The aim was to provide a professional networking group dedicated to Executive Assistants (EAs), Personal Assistants (PAs), Secretaries and Administrators – in other words, all admin professionals. The network provides an opportunity for members to connect with like-minded individuals from across different sectors based in Exeter and the surrounding areas, providing a forum to share best practice, enabling all members to be the best they can be.

Initially, the network organized two evening development events a year. This then expanded to some ad hoc social events, and then some venue visits were added. Now, it also hosts monthly business breakfasts, an annual conference and ad hoc workshops.

Its mission is to raise the profile of admin roles, as well as deliver fresh and forward-thinking training, recognizing the changes made to the PA role in recent years.

In 2016, the group's development theme was around 'Brand', with their first event focusing on personal branding, and their second event focusing on building an online brand

and engagement. In 2017 they are looking at the changing world of work. In their first event they looked at the macro trends of urbanization, demography, life expectancy, the ever-increasing capability of technology and what this could mean for PAs and their careers. Their second event was about sharing tips with members on how to build mental toughness and resilience, to help them deal with the ever-increasing pace of change in the world of work.

The monthly breakfasts have speakers from the local business community, aimed at developing members' awareness of businesses they and their organizations could work with, as well as developments and challenges in the market.

The annual conference has four keynote speakers, and networking opportunities, as well as industry-related exhibitors.

There are no membership fees, but the group charges a nominal fee for the breakfast meetings and development events. Initially the group had no budget at all, and relied on negotiating deals with venues and speakers – highlighting the benefits to both of being able to showcase their offerings to such an influential group. After all, it's generally the PAs who book venues and have the ear of the senior leadership team and are therefore able to promote suppliers into their own organizations. Kim kept a 'portfolio of wins' – so each time a speaker or a venue got a booking as a result of working with the network, this was recorded. If one PA introduced business to another PA's organization, this was also recorded. This built up very quickly, and is a useful tool in presenting a business case to venues, speakers and sponsors when negotiating deals. The amount of business being introduced by PAs to other organizations was quickly noticed by members' employers and local businesses and helped in raising the profile of the group, as well as in gaining employers' support for PAs to attend events.

As Kim's ambitions for the Network grew, and she needed more support for running and funding the group's activities and promotion, she was joined by her colleague, Rebecca Eccles. Rebecca complemented Kim's skills and provided different perspectives, ensuring that the events and development opportunities offered were attractive to a broad audience. Kim also secured some sponsorship funding and marketing support from her employer.

The group's profile and membership continued to grow, and soon outgrew the support Kim's employers were able to provide. This created an opportunity for Kim to set up a dedicated website for the network, and to put the network on a more formal footing by incorporating it as a limited company. This has been a steep learning curve for Kim and Rebecca, but one they have benefitted from and enjoyed.

The group is now actively seeking corporate sponsorship to ensure its sustainability. Kim continues to work full-time as an executive assistant to the managing partner at a large regional law firm, and has outsourced marketing and some admin support for the network to local providers. The group is regularly featured in the local press.

A focus of the network is to raise the profile of the PA profession and the network's individual members. To this end, the group held a development session with a business coach, who helped the group with building confidence, and provided members with tools to ask for the recognition and reward they deserved within their own organizations. Kim also persuaded a local business publication to feature a 'PA of the Month', which enabled a number of members to showcase their role and the organization they work for. Members were also encouraged to become more active on social media – again to raise their profiles – and this was supported by a number of 'point and click' workshops on Twitter and LinkedIn where members brought their own devices and were shown everything from how to set up their profiles to posting their first tweet.

At one event the group were joined by an Executive PA Magazine PA of the Year award winner, who talked about their experience of winning an award, and the difference it had made to them and their career. Members were then encouraged to put themselves forward for various awards and, as a result, the group now has a number of award-winning PAs amongst its membership. Members have also secured places on committees organizing awards as well as speaking engagements.

Exeter is an ambitious city, with its business leaders keen to work together to build a world-class workforce. The Exeter PA Network is keen to play a part in this, understanding that businesses require talented and engaged admin staff to support growth. This is reflected in the quality and content of its development events designed to up-skill the local talent pool. The group has also held a showcase event to which it invited senior leaders, L&D and HR Directors, to demonstrate how the Network is supporting local businesses and how their PAs, and therefore their organizations, are benefitting from taking part.

Raising the profile of individual PAs and their roles nationally via PA award ceremonies supports Exeter's efforts to showcase the quality of business being undertaken in the city, demonstrating that it can compete on the national and international stage.

A number of recruiting managers at local organizations, as well as recruitment agencies, now ask job applicants if they are a member of the network as part of the recruitment process. This demonstrates that employers now recognize that a PA who is part of the network will add even more value to their organization.

Kim is a member of the regional advisory board of the UK's national association for the PA profession, EPAA (Executive and Personal Assistant Association). Kim is working with the CEO of EPAA to host a summit for regional PA network leads across the UK, to offer support and share best practice, and to ensure the sustainability of these important resources for all PAs.

Contact Exeter PA Network through the following channels:

W: www.exeterpanetwork.com
E: hello@exeterpanetwork.com
Twitter: @ExeterPANetwork
Facebook: https://en-gb.facebook.com/ExeterPANetwork/
LinkedIn: https://www.linkedin.com groups/Exeter-PA-Network-5092593/about

Case study 3

The Discovery PA Centre of Excellence

by Cathy Harris

Back in 2001, I, together with a group of other Discovery PAs, decided that we needed a resource centre to refer to for all our work-related efforts. There were so many processes and rules, policies and templates, and it appeared that every PA had a different version of everything, stored neatly in their own individual folders on their desktops. It became messy. We weren't talking to each other and it seemed like every assistant was working independently from the rest of her peers in our organization, and to make matters worse, our company was growing at a rate of approximately 100 new employees every month!

It was at this juncture that a handful of us decided to create a space where we could communicate one standard which was in line with our corporate identity and brand as an organization, and so our PA forum was born.

It was a lot of hard work; we had to collate and update policies and procedures and all the templates that went with them. It was a time of discovery and trying new things, of networking with peers we had only previously seen in passing in the passageways. It was a time of awakening and a birth of a whole new adventure that became the benchmark for many internal networks in South Africa.

I cannot lie to you, it was difficult trying to get buy-in from many PAs themselves – change was always a challenge, but as we progressed, and as those who did participate started reaping the rewards of being ahead of their game and being informed, it wasn't long before the masses followed, and we had a steady flow of believers and participants.

Managers took even longer to buy into the idea, saying that we were a "union", or a "clan", and it took a lot of consistent hard work and innovation to market the idea and the initiatives to them, and in 2006 we were given a budget to work from.

By 2012 we were on the map, respected and applauded for our efforts, with ongoing in-house training initiatives, networking events and get-to-know sessions. It was during the latter part of 2014 that things took a nosedive because of one assistant who told her executive we were a waste of time… Yes, it took just one, and for almost two years the PA forum went into hibernation.

In 2016 I decided enough was enough and set about re-initiating the forum, with proposal after proposal to reignite the concept that I know adds so much value. It was hard work and I did get emails saying I was "flogging a dead horse", but I never gave up, and finally in 2016, with the help of many phenomenal assistants, the Discovery PA Centre of Excellence was born. We are still in business and even stronger than before!

On the 18th of May 2017 I did a little calculation on the ROI (Return on Interest) that the PA Centre of Excellence has saved the organization JUST on training over a period of 8 years…. The result was over R7million (£437500.00; $540000.00), and this calculated at the bare minimum cost – an external training vendor would have been double the cost. So there you go. Make your mark and leave a legacy!

The Discovery PA Network

Case Study 4

The National Health Service Wales PA Network

by Catherine Thomas

Catherine has been involved with this network for the last 10 years. Starting off with a very limited budget and about 30 PAs, they now have over 400 PAs registered and are likely to be among the largest organizational PA networks in Europe.

Catherine organizes two conferences a year and sends out a newsletter every other month. For her it has been an absolute joy and a nightmare all at the same time, and I know this feeling of overwhelming anxiety, when you still have a full time career and you commit yourself to your profession on such a large scale – it is very scary and not for the faint-hearted!

Having recently changed roles she feels the time has come to hand over the network to someone else at the NHS. She has learnt a lot and gained so much confidence in running the network over the years. This is her story.

Here's how the idea of the NHS Wales PA network has developed from its start to the present day. Given all the mountains I have climbed and seas I've swum in and nearly drowned, it hasn't all been plain sailing, there have been hiccups along the way but there have been some great moments.

I was, and in fact still am, a true PA. I say "was" because I am slowly moving out of the role and more into projects. However being a PA is my default mode and whatever happens either it will find me or I will find it! I'm in that awkward situation at the moment of trying to find my Director, who I have been with for 15 odd years, a new PA so I can concentrate on project work, but the boss and I are finding our bond a hard habit to break!

I joined the NHS in Wales as a temp back in 2005 covering annual leave for the Chief Executive's PAs. I did my stint, left, got called back and am still there.

I spent a while developing my role, my knowledge and gaining confidence before I started to get itchy feet and felt I needed something new. A flyer arrived on my desk for a PA conference in London and I thought why not? This was back in 2007, not many conferences around at that time for PAs. That conference changed my life, and I very much hope that this book does the same for you. At that conference was Susie Barron-Stubley (who we have since sadly lost) and Vanessa Price (who had won a PA Award a year or so before). So inspired was I, I remember what they talked about – Vanessa about the PA Award and what winning has done for her and Susie asked why PAs didn't talk to each other. We, as PAs, know a lot of stuff which we don't share. She had a point. I was so inspired by Susie that on my trip back to Wales, I wrote a business plan on scrappy bits of paper to start our own PA network. We had six PAs in our building. We could do this.

So the following day in I go to my Director, Sally. Sally and I have worked on and off together for 15 years and she is hugely supportive of me and of the PA Network. I put forward my idea and she didn't bat an eyelid – yes, go for it she said, BUT you need a challenge for your appraisal so instead of launching the network just in the building, go NHS Wales wide.

That threw me for a moment – there are 17,000 admin people in NHS Wales. It's the country's largest employer.

Note that they aren't all secretaries/PAs, they cover all sorts of roles.

I took the challenge once my heart rate had returned to normal. For those that don't know Wales very well it is four hours in a car from North to South, heavily populated in some areas around the coast and not so much in others.

I contacted a few of the PAs I knew (they now form my committee). We talked over the idea and thankfully they didn't think I was mad. We talked about what a network would bring to the NHS PAs and about launching with a conference. We got Susie Barron-Stubley to Wales to talk through the idea and we were all systems go. We drew up a list of the PAs we all knew – which came to about 40.

Now I had to organize a conference. I had to ask for some money for a venue. Sally, my Director, said ask Andy the Finance Director – you might need to write a business case, she said. OK, challenge number two. Now, like you I had typed and formatted many a business case in my role but writing one myself was a new one on me. It took me hours, but I did it and submitted it to the Director of Finance. He said yes, no questions asked. In fact his words were "I would have said yes without the business case".

I had to tell these 40 PAs what we were doing, I needed to sell the idea of a network and explain the benefits. Tell them what they were going to get out of it. These days this is a hundred times easier as networks are more common – PA networks are popping up all over the place.

So, I organized a distribution list on Outlook for the 40 PAs and wrote a newsletter. Nice and friendly, explaining the concept and hoping they would get on board with it. On the whole feedback was really positive, I wasn't mad after all – then I got a negative email. Believe it or not, it was sent by a PA as a 'reply to all', which obviously came back to me. This is the one email that I come back to every time I do something – what if I get another of one of these? Am I being too big for my boots, am I getting carried away? That email totally floored me. And I could have jacked the whole thing in at that point. It would have been really easy to say 'forget it'. But those who know me know that I don't allow myself to stay at the bottom for long and I bounce back harder and faster.

For the first few years I held the conference in Mid-Wales, thinking that everyone can get there as it's the middle for everyone. We had 60 attend the first ever conference (nine years ago now). The only marketing I do is via word of mouth – every time I send out a newsletter numbers go up. But as the years went on the conference numbers were reducing as staff couldn't get the OK to attend training sessions. Trying to get speakers to the middle of nowhere, no matter how pretty it was, was also no mean feat either!

So I made the decision to split the conference to north and south Wales, but that meant I needed more money. I had a small budget that just about paid for the venue, lunch and really reduced speaker costs. I knew that my organization wouldn't be able to fund two conferences, so what to do? I wrote another paper and presented it to the Workforce and Organizational Development Directors (HR in simple terms) to ask them to fund the conferences. Much, much harder than the first paper I had to write, as I didn't know half of the Directors and this was a new concept to them, so it was in the lap of the gods. I did prime every one of their PAs beforehand mind you!

Another yes without question. My budget had doubled overnight. I now just about break even every year. It's not much, especially when you are hiring venues for over 100 people, but I manage to do it year on year – I came in within 2p last year! I feel I am an expert in doing conferences on the cheap!

I write a newsletter to the network every other month when the daytime job allows. I don't write more than a couple of pages, I have always wanted it to be an easy read that you can dip in and out of. I share latest PA news, conferences such as EPAAs, ExecSecLive, the Office and PA Show, I share Microsoft tips and PA stories; how dirty keyboards are, that sort of thing. This gets circulated to the NHS Wales PAs along with friends of the network and I am more than happy to share this with you if you would like it. Your lives will never be the same again...

Feeling that the Conferences needed a bit of buzz, I started the NHS PA Award looking for the best PA working in the NHS in Wales. Invitations were invited from Directors, Line Managers, Chairs and Chief Executives across the NHS. Numbers are slowly rising and the Directors seem to take great delight in secretly nominating their PAs from their home address so as to not get caught out. I often get email apologies for the formatting of the application, they don't know how to do it themselves! I see some quite amazing applications for PAs going way over their job descriptions. Some real unsung heroes. The winner and runner up are announced at the conference by whichever NHS Wales Chief Executive is on the agenda. They love doing it, and the PAs hate the attention.

I mentioned Vanessa Price earlier, who had won a PA Award. She got me thinking: if she won an award, why can't I? So a few years later I applied and was runner up in the Times/Hays competition. At the time, this was the only PA Award in existence – now there are many.

There is nothing better than hearing from a PA after the conference that says "because of you I've enrolled on a course or asked for training". A few years ago I asked people to submit their interest in attending Lucy Brazier's

Executive Secretary LIVE. Claire Power was the lucky PA who got a place.

I am not going to tell you that running a network is easy because it isn't. It wouldn't be fair to tell you otherwise. It is time consuming, it's hard work, and the buck, in the main, stops with you. If you are considering starting up a network then I urge you to go ahead. All it needs is a few like-minded people to get together over coffee and a biscuit to talk about the difficulties in managing more than one Director, for example, and your network is born. Once you have a few of these meetings under your belt and your colleagues have realized that you aren't going to make them do a song and dance routine then that is the time to aim bigger.

My top tips for starting a network are:

- Get together a bunch of like-minded people – come up with a timeline and a plan of action (i.e. conference next May, lunchtime learning session every other Monday).

- Write a paper to Directors to explain what you are doing – you will get buy-in from them if they know what you are doing.

- Ask the Director of Finance for a small budget to cover costs of speakers. If you don't ask you don't get.

- Write a newsletter/blog to let PAs know what you are doing – expect some hostility. There is always a PA who knows everything and thinks networks are a waste of time. They will come round eventually, don't try to crack them.

- Networks can be done on a budget: you don't need hotels; bring your own biscuits; use your contacts to speak (perhaps a colleague in IT; a PA who knows all the shortcuts on Word; an HR contact keen on Change Management or stress signs). Once you've got some confidence then go to network leaders and they will come to speak for a low charge (normally just transport costs).

- Meetings can be as long or as short as you need; whole day, half day or lunchtime. If you are starting off then perhaps lunch and learns are better to start with.

- Start small and build – your confidence will grow.

- Make sure PAs (and their bosses) know that it is a network to learn and you are all in it together – there is a coordinator but no 'boss'. You need to word this carefully as people will ask "who does she think she is?" – they need to be aware that you are all learning together and from each other and it isn't you training them.

- Ask PAs what subjects they want to learn about – but be warned, you might need to tell them because they don't know what they don't know!

- Try not to cancel events – people lose faith.

- At the end of the year write a report to show Directors what the network has done, what sessions were held and how far the network has gone. I did one recently and sent it to the Minister of Health – and I got a letter back. Promote yourself and the network!

7

Examples and Samples

In this chapter I have provided you with document examples, samples and other things you may feel you need when putting all the pieces of your internal network together. I hope that you will find this useful, and you have my permission to copy it!

Example of a proposal document

The document prepared below is an example of how to put forward your proposal to your management team. They will want to know what the core purpose is, what kind of governance it will apply, your main initiatives you will want to host etc. It is pretty self-explanatory and you can bespoke it for your needs.

Ideally this document should be laid out as a proposal document, with a professional front page with your organization's logo, or a logo you as a team have designed for your network. Make it look professional, and make sure that all the contents are purposeful.

Proposal to initiate an Internal Assistant Network

Dated...

Presented to the Executive Team

Core Purpose

The internal network will provide access to essential resources required by the PAs on mandatory operational procedures pertinent to their roles. The internal network will provide a platform for PAs to access training and developmental needs which will be standardized across the board, giving access to training and development to all PAs. Lastly, the internal network will provide a fair and equitable opportunity for our organization's assistants to be accountable for their profession by participating in the Internal-Network-organized workgroups and the initiatives derived from it, in a positive and constructive manner.

1. Governance

The internal network is open to all PAs within the organization, including all regions and branches, and will be run by the PAs for the PAs, championed by the organization's Human Resources Division.

Participation in the internal network workgroup is voluntary. A chairperson will be nominated on an annual basis by the internal network workgroup assistant community.

The internal network will operate in a transparent manner and in line with the organization's core values. All views and contributions made to the workgroup by the assistant community will be considered by the workgroup in line with the organization's core values and the purpose of the internal network.

Workgroup meetings will be recorded and minutes of meetings will be made available on the internal network folder to view by the internal network community. Meetings will take place during working hours.

A budget for the internal network has been created and will fall under the organization's Human Resources Division. Access will be provided to the internal network community to view this document.

2. Training And Development

The internal network will focus on the following training and developmental initiatives for all PAs.

2.1 PA Induction Program

The Assistant Induction will be mandatory for all new PAs and optional for existing PAs requiring refresher training, on a monthly basis, and will include facilitation from business owners. Processes which are essential to the PA's job function will include:

2.1.1   Recruitment
2.1.2   Procurement
2.1.3   Stationery Tool
2.1.4   Travel
2.1.5   Payroll and Reimbursements

2.1.6   Information Technology and the Intranet
2.1.7   Learner Management Systems
2.1.8   Introduction to the Internal Network

2.2 Training Courses

- Organization-recommended accredited secretarial training courses and seminars.

- In-house Internal-Network-facilitated training sessions.

- Encouragement of online training provided by the organization.

- Organization Assistant Conference – to be hosted on an annual basis.

2.3 Mentoring and coaching

Senior PAs within the organization have both the skills and ability to assist in the mentoring and coaching of entry-level and less experienced PAs into the secretarial profession, as well as any other assistant requesting mentorship. This initiative will be voluntary. A resource tool has been created and has been used successfully on PAs in the past.

3. Operational Resources

3.1 The Internal Network Folder

The folder is in the process of being created, and will be available to the assistant community. Resources will include the following and remains open for any additional resources that you may require:

- Recruitment templates and updated recruitment process information;

- Procurement processes and Walton's stationery tool guide;

- Meeting room information and contact details;

- PA contact lists and departmental information;

- Travel information, policies and templates;

- LMS process and guidelines;

- Preferred suppliers list;

- Standard templates for agenda, minutes and matters arising;

- Call logging guide;

- Training calendar;

- Event management guidelines, process and contact details;

- Links to other company managed templates and forms;

- The internal network champions and assistant contact and information list.

3.2 Business Knowledge Sessions

These will be sessions hosted by the internal network on new initiatives by the business which need to be communicated to the assistant community and will happen as and when the need arises.

3.3 Network Opportunities

The internal network workgroup will provide opportunities for the assistant community to network amongst each other in order to build strong relationships, gain insight into the cross-culture of the organization and to ensure a team effort is achieved. This can be done through organizing:

- Secretaries Day event;

- Incentive programs based on your participation in training and development initiatives;

- Annual Assistant Conference.

EXAMPLES AND SAMPLES

Template 1

Operating framework for the internal network

This example is to justify the reason why a budget is required, and should illustrate key stakeholders and beneficiaries of the internal network, who are the organization's and our leadership (managers and executives).

FRAMEWORK

- ✓ To provide the assistant community with essential operational resourcing tools pertinent to the job.

- ✓ To ensure that the assistant community is informed, trained and kept updated with changes and processes that occur within the business.

- ✓ To provide access to secretarial training and development opportunities relative to their job functions.

- ✓ To provide the opportunity for PAs to be actively accountable participants in their profession and effectively support the organization's leadership.

- ✓ To ensure the internal network is championed by an appropriate organizational department and executive.

Key Process Owners: Once the internal network has been approved by the executive team, invitations to participate in the workgroup will go out to the assistant community, and roles will be allocated.

Investment: based on headcount of, for example in this case, 133 assistants.

Governance investment includes stationery, branding, refreshments, strategy session venues, hotel accommodation, vehicle hire for distant delegates, and speaker costs where applicable.

Key to Role Matrix

P = Primary owner, S = Secondary owner/s, C = Contributory

KEY PROCESS DRIVERS	FUNCTIONS / DESCRIPTION	ROLE MATRIX					FREQUENCY				INVESTMENT*
		EXCO Champion	Workgroup	Chairperson	Key Process Owners*	PA Community	Monthly	Quarterly	Bi-Annually	Annually	
GOVERNANCE	Open to all assistants in the company					P					
	Run by the assistants for the assistants		P	S		C					
	[EXCO / executive] will be Internal Network Champion	P	S			C					
	Mandatory (or voluntary) for all assistants to participate in internal network initiatives		P	S		C					
	Workgroup participation voluntary		P	S		C					
	Chairperson nominated by Assistant Community		S	P		C					
	Invitation extended to all Discovery Assistants to participate on the workgroup committee		P	S	Workgroup and Chairperson	C					
	Operate in a transparent manner		S	P		C					R60 000
	All meetings will be recorded and minutes of meetings made available to the Assistant Community and Champion.		S	P							
	All contributions received from the Assistant Community will be considered in line with our key objectives.		P	S		C					
	Annual report to be compiled for the EXCO Champion and for financial auditing purposes.		S	P		C					
	Assistant Internal Network meetings	C	P	S		C					
	Assistant Network strategy sessions	C	P	S		C					
	Effectively manage Assistant Network budget	C	S	S	P						
TRAINING AND DEVELOP-MENT	**PA Induction** Mandatory for all new assistants. Optional for existing assistants Recruitment / resignation process Procurement process Stationery ordering tool Travel process Payroll and reimbursement process Technology infrastructure and Intranet In-house Learner Management Systems training, if applicable Internal Network events and social functions		S	S	P	C					No Cost to Assistant Network

	Secretarial Training										
	National framework accredited training courses and workshops		S	S	P	C					R200 000
	Bespoke National Certificate in Business Administration Certification		S	S	P	C					R100 000
	In-house business and production information sessions		S	S	P	C					No cost
	Organization's in-house online training initiatives		S	S	P	C		As and when required			No direct cost
	Internal Network run training workshops for assistants, facilitated by assistants		S	S	P	C					No cost
	Annual Internal Network Conference or Summit, which may include international and national subject facilitators.	C	S	S	P	C					R220 000
	Mentoring and Coaching Provided by senior assistants		S	S	P	C		As and when required			No cost
OPERATIONAL RESOURCING	**Internal Network Folder on DNA** Updated Discovery Group electronic letterheads		S	S	P	C					
	Forex templates and financial process information		S	S	P	C					
	Recruitment templates and updated recruitment process information		S	S	P	C					
	Resignation templates and updated resignation process information		S	S	P	C					
	Procurement order request forms, BEE compliance and process information		S	S	P	C					
	Discovery group office maps		S	S	P	C					
	Meeting room booking process, information and contact details		S	S	P	C					
	PA contact lists, companies and departmental information		S	S	P	C		Maintained on an ongoing basis.			No Cost
	Travel processes, policies, templates and information		S	S	P	C					
	LMS process and guidelines		S	S	P	C					
	Preferred supplier lists		S	S	P	C					
	Stationery tool guide		S	S	P	C					
	Standard Discovery agenda, minutes and matters arising templates		S	S	P	C					
	Group Facilities templates, guidelines and procedures		S	S	P	C					
	Call logging process guide		S	S	P	C					
	Training and development initiatives		S	S	P	C					
	Event management guidelines, processes and information		S	S	P	C					
	Internal Network information				P	C					
									TOTAL INVESTMENT		**R630 000.00**

87

Template 2

Project Plan

This example is to help you and your team to plot out everything that needs to be accomplished within a certain period of time, with initiatives allocated to owners with the required action that needs to take place. A project plan needs to be a working document, which should be updated as and when necessary to keep the workgroup informed of progress. I would recommend the project plan be saved on Dropbox and all workgroup members be given access to update their portions accordingly. That way you do not need to update multiple inputs.

The idea here is to keep it simple and to the point. When you set up yours please also add a "Progress" column into your worksheet. Under the "Action by" column put the person's name.

ACTIVITY	REQUIREMENT	ACTION BY	START DATE	END DATE
Proposal to management	1. Proposal to be finalized and approved by Champion or HR Department.	Initiator EXCO Member Internal Network Champion		
Approval from EXCO	1. Ready to be presented to Holdings EXCO	Champion Director		
Invitation to assistants to participate in initiative	1. Meeting invitation to be sent to the assistant community inviting participation on workgroup	Initiator		
Set up formal workgroup	1. Invite take up of various roles within the workgroup and appoint / vote for chairperson	Initiator		
Update assistants' email list	1. Ensure the Assistant Contact list is updated with all Discovery PAs including DFC's 2. Ensure outlook distribution list is updated in line with contact list	Workgroup		
Hosting of first workgroup committee meeting	1. Meeting invitation to be sent to volunteers 2. Agenda to be compiled at the meeting to plan a strategy session as soon as possible 3. Decide on date for strategy session	Initiator Workgroup members		

Communication to the organization's assistant community	1. An email to be prepared and sent to the assistant community announcing the workgroup members and requesting votes for the workgroup chairperson 2. The chairperson will be notified by the workgroup and communicated to the assistant community in January 2012	Individual who does not want to stand for chairperson to prepare and receive votes for the role.
First chaired meeting	1. Plan for strategy session agenda 2. Agenda to include budget proposal preparation 3. Agenda to include proposed initiatives for the year 4. Confirm date and venue	Workgroup members
Strategy session	1. Workgroup to work through program for the year	Workgroup members
Implementation of projects	1. Induction training 2. PA Folder 3. Initiatives planned for the year 4. Budget proposal preparation	Workgroup to decide on and allocate initiatives to owners

Template 3

Welcome Letter

Dear Assistant

On behalf of the Internal Network Workgroup Committee we would like to welcome you to [organization's name, or a name you have decided on for your network].

We are very proud indeed to be able to facilitate an internal network that will provide you the assistant with all the resources, assistance and support you will need to work alongside the leadership of our organization in an efficient, effective and professional manner, ensuring that we exceed their expectations in delivering the best possible quality service.

The focus of our internal network is to empower and inspire our assistant network to deliver dazzling service with passion. As a [organization's name] assistant you will also be given the opportunity to take charge of your own personal development and growth within our great organization, and enjoy the positive cameraderie and support we all currently enjoy.

We look forward to meeting you at the next [Network's name] Induction program, and subsequent networking and learning initiatives.

Kind regards,

[Name of chairperson]
Chairperson: [Network Name]

STRATEGY SESSION WORKBOOK

1. Getting Started

Notes:

2. Why would we want an internal network in our organization?

3. Forming a Committee

(a) Who should be included in the internal network?
(b) How will the committee be selected?
(c) Who should lead?
(d) How should we organise Corporate Governance within the internal network?
(e) What should we expect in terms of attendance?

4. Setting Standards

Although many organizations already have set standards in place for certain operational requirements there are, however, gaps where it is important, for both the image and the efficiency of the business, to have set standards pertaining to various functions required to be carried out by the PA as part of her or his job function. Often what happens is that rules are set and filed away, or only certain departments or people are aware of these standards, which are not effectively communicated to the people at ground level – mainly the assistant community. We need to look therefore at what standards we want to set. There are plenty of them, but what I can suggest is that you select those which are pertinent and important to you for now and build on it as you go. You and your committee can create a manual of the standards set later.

What standards would we like to include?

---

5. Networking

One of the most important characteristics we need as a PA or office professional is the ability to be able to communicate. We cannot grow or develop if we don't communicate, we cannot express opinion or give advice if we are not informed, and above all, we cannot be effective if we don't know about our own organization or the career which we are pursuing.

The following network activities can be included:

6. Training and Development

We often overlook our own development in the quest to manage our positions and carry out our day-to-day functions within the time limits we have, something which for most of us can often be quite difficult. However one advantage of having an internal network within your organization will be to help you make an informed decision on the right choice of training for our profession.

The idea is twofold though: firstly, when you receive external notification for relevant PA training, this can be reviewed by the internal network committee and then circulated to the rest of the PAs if appropriate. The network will serve as the main point of communication on training and development for the PA. The other side of this is to consider, depending on the size of your organization, the creation of a PA Induction Program for new PAs who have recently joined, or PAs who have been with the organization for some time, but need to brush up on their general knowledge of the organization.

Actions to consider for training and development:

_____

_____

_____

_____

_____

_____

_____

_____

7. Special Events

One of the main functions for the internal network will be to plan and co-ordinate the special events that could happen within the organization. These could include the following events / special occasions:

_____

_____

_____

_____

_____

_____

_____

8. Shopping Lists

A shopping list can consist of the following items:

---

9. Information Folders

As we have progressed through some of the many ideas and concepts for our internal network, we now need to establish an accessible central hub for all our information, ensuring that it is accessible to all our PAs. How do we do this?

10. Marketing the Internal Network

We have now established a basic foundation for the core purpose and reasons for having an internal network within the organization, but how do we sell this idea, how do we get buy-in from our managers and how do we get the other PAs in our organization to participate?

11. Working on a Budget

It is important, but not absolutely necessary, to have a budget from which to work. Most organizations do set aside a budget facility for training purposes for their employees. It may be a good idea to establish what this budget is and to use it to form your own internal network budget.

Steps to take will include the following ideas:

12. Roles and Responsibilities

We have now worked through most of the detail, but in order to bring this all together we need to ensure that the operational side of our new forum is taken care of and the administration functions and the role of each of the committee members will be effectively managed.

(a) Chairperson:

_____

(b) Secretary:

_____

(c) Team Members:

_____

_____

_____

_____

_____

_____

_____

8

Conclusion:
The Value of an Internal Network

When my colleagues and I at Discovery started our internal network over 16 years ago, we had absolutely no idea of the impact this movement would have on our peers or our organization. It was like planting a seed and knowing it will grow with maintenance, but not fully understanding how BIG this idea would grow. Yes, risky, but we need to take risks to discover the beauty of the legacy trail we create.

I knew that our growing problems could be resolved if all the PAs were efficiently equipped with the right resources and the correct information, had easy access to these processes, and at the same time were able to build on an intellectual wellness where we could provide training and development opportunities for our peers to grow and add value to their own personal contributions and that of the organization.

Communicating this was a long process of preparation and planning, putting forward proposals, gathering the troops to form a workgroup of assistants to run and maintain the initiative, and then finally presenting it to our executive and management teams, but it was worth it. I know for certain that we have contributed to there being less stress and anxiety amongst our peers, that there exists a sense of pride and belonging, workloads are streamlined and more efficient, communication between assistants, managers and stakeholders is constantly taking place, our peers are developing their skills and careers and there is a sense of unity and work satisfaction.

The culture within our organization is extremely innovative and results driven, and because of these factors having an internal network takes some of the immediate pressures of work off an individual, because we know we have a one-stop resource and help centre to back us up, and provide us with the right resources to get the job done.

We have a WhatsApp group where all our assistants are engaged, and at any given time during the course of a working day various assistants call out for help, and get assisted almost immediately! This is one of many initiatives which drives wellness and peace of mind in our busy workplace.

Wellness presents itself in many forms, not just physically, but also psychologically, spiritually, emotionally, intellectually, occupationally and socially. All of these dimensions play a pivotal role in how we perform and contribute to our careers and society. In today's busy, challenging, stressful and high-pressure workplace the value of an Internal PA Network to the wellness of all assistants in an organisation cannot be overstated!

Appendix:
Extending your Network

Once you have your internal network up and running, the networking does not stop there! In order to continue to grow and expand you have to integrate your internal network with external networks. The reason for this is to ensure that the educational and developmental aspects of networking are not just limited to internal boundaries, but rather can expand and be exploited beyond what you just do at your own organizations.

The best way to do this is to connect, join up with and become members of networks and associations which are specific to our profession. So be careful. In South Africa for instance, there is an association that caters for all support staff and administrators – this is not necessarily where you want to connect, however, so there is a learning opportunity that exists there too.

We have to appreciate that our profession as management assistants has evolved. Yes, some of you call yourselves admins, PAs, executive PAs etc, but ultimately we are, by all measures, management assistants, as we assist management! We do not necessarily just do administrative tasks anymore, but we are also strategic partners with our managers and their teams.

When we are able to identify with the value we add to our profession, we also realize the value in being connected globally to other management assistant networks and associations.

There is HUGE value to be gained in becoming members of the various global networks. Not only do you get the opportunity to participate in training and development opportunities, but you also have the added advantage of participating on their various committees and councils. These additional "extramural" professional participation endeavours can be added to your resume, and will stand you in good stead as being recognized as going beyond the ordinary and participating in being extraordinary!

Here is my list of personal bests (courtesy of Executive Secretary Magazine), so go ahead and invest in becoming an active participant, or member or subscriber. There are tons to choose from; don't necessarily be limited by country – let us think global!

(Do however make sure that you check the various organizations' websites for updated names and other details, as this is a dynamic list and, while accurate at time of going to press, will be constantly changing in the future.)

Enjoy!

COUNTRY	NETWORK / ASSOCIATION	WEBSITE ADDRESS	CONTACT NAME/S
ASIA	CIPD, Asia (Chartered Institute of Personnel and Development)	www.cipd.asia	Franc Gooding
AUSTRALIA	AIOP – Australian Institute of Office Professionals – Mildura	www.aiop.com.au	
AUSTRALIA	AIOP – Australian Institute of Office Professionals – National	www.aiop.com.au	Sue McComasky – National President
AUSTRALIA	AIOP – Australian Institute of Office Professionals – NSW	www.aiop.com.au	Melissa Macri – President
AUSTRALIA	AIOP – Australian Institute of Office Professionals – NT	www.aiop.com.au	Christine Heness – President
AUSTRALIA	AIOP – Australian Institute of Office Professionals – QLD	www.aiop.com.au	
AUSTRALIA	AIOP – Australian Institute of Office Professionals – SA	www.aiop.com.au	Kristen Mackenzie – President Annick Boeynaems

AUSTRALIA	AIOP – Australian Institute of Office Professionals – VIC	www.aiop.com.au	Elvira Mazza – President
AUSTRALIA	AIOP – Australian Institute of Office Professionals – WA	www.aiop.com.au	Shervaun Steenson – President
AUSTRALIA	EAN – Executive Assistant Network	www.executiveassistant.com	
BARBADOS	Barbados Association of Office Professionals (BAOP)	www.baop.org	
BELGIUM	ALISAD – Association Liégeoise des Secrétaires et Assistant(e)s de Direction	www.alisad.eu	Estelle Dejasse
BELGIUM	IMA, Belgium	www.be.ima-network.org	San Cools – Chairperson
BELGIUM	ManAs – Antwerp Network for Management Assistants	www.manas.be	Annick Boeynaems

BRAZIL	ABPSEC – Brazilian Association of Research in Secretarial Science	www.abpsec.com.br	Emili Martins – President
BRAZIL	FENASSEC – Brazil's National Federation of Secretaries	www.fenassec.com.br	Maria Bernadette Lira Lieuthier – President
BRAZIL	Pepitas Secretaries Club	www.pepitassecretariesclub.com	Pepita Soler
BRAZIL	Sindicato das Secretárias e Secretários do Estado de São Paulo (SINSESP)	www.sinsesp.com.br	Isabel Baptista – President Eduardo Souza – Assistant
BRAZIL	SISERGS – Sindicato das Secretrias e Secretarios no estdo do Rio Grande do Sul	www.sisergs.com.br	Nubia Martins – President
CANADA	Association of Administrative Assistants	www.aaa.ca	
CANADA	Canadian Association oF Virtual Assistants	www.canadianava.org	Elayne Whitfield
CANADA	Exceptional EA	www.exceptionalea.com	Shelagh Donnelly

CANADA	Federation Des Secretaires Professionnelles du Quebec (FSPQ)	www.fspq.qc.ca	
CANADA	IAAP – International Association of Administrative Professional s	www.iaap-hq.org	Rachel Reynolds
EUROPE	IMA	www.ima-network.org	
FINLAND	IMA, Finland	www.fi.ima-network.org	Anne Kangasniemi – Chairman
FINLAND	Sihteeriyhdistys Sekreterarföreningen ry	www.sihteeriyhdistys.fi	
FRANCE	IMA, France	www.fr.ima-network.org	Lizzie Jean-Nandjui – Acting Chairman
FRANCE	FFMAS, France (French Federation of Trade of the Assistantship and Secretariat)	www.ffmas.com	Annie Gonod

GABON	FFMAS, Gabon (French Federation of Trade of the Assistantship and Secretariat)	www.ffmas.com/qui-sommes-nous=cartographie-du-reseau/153-pays-francophones-44-club-privilege.html	Marie-Yvonne Okome Essone
GERMANY	Bundesverband Sekretariat und Büromanagement e.V. (bSb)	www.bsb-office.de	
GERMANY	IMA, Germany	www.de.ima-network.org	Vera Berndt – Chairman
GHANA	The Professional Secretaries Association of Ghana (PROSAG)		Rosemary Ackah
GLOBAL	Be the Ultimate Assistant	www.bonnielowkramen.com	Bonnie Low-Kramen
GLOBAL	GEA – Global Executive Assistants	www.globalexecutiveassistants.com	
GLOBAL	Office Dynamics International	www.officedynamics.com	Jasmine Freeman
CYPRUS	IMA, Cyprus	www.cy.ima-network.org	Agathi Konizou – Chairman

GREECE	IMA, Greece	www.gr.ima-network.org	Piyi Ghini-Simacou – Chairman
GUERNSEY	Guernsey PA Connect	www.guernseypaconnect.com	Donna Olliver, Caroline Renouf
ICELAND	IMA, Iceland	www.is.ima-network.org	Guorun Erla Leifsdottir
INDIA	IASAP – Indian Association of Secretaries & Administrative Professionals	www.iasapindia.com	Sharon Pires – Chairman
IRELAND	APAI – Association of PAs in Ireland	www.apai.ie/index.html	Aideen
IRELAND	CIPD, Ireland (Chartered Institute of Personnel and Development)	www.cipd.co.uk/global/europe/irland	
ITALY	IMA, Italy	www.it.ima-network.org	Silvia Salomon – Chairman
ITALY	MACSE Italia – Manager Assistant Carriera Sviluppo Evoluzione	www.macseitalia.it	MariaChiara Novati
ITALY	Secretary.IT Manager Assistant Network	www.secretary.it	Vania Alessi

JAMAICA	Jamaica Association of Secretaries & Administrative Professionals (JASAP)	www.jasap-online.org	
JAPAN	JSA – Japan Secretaries & Administrative Professionals Association	www.hishokyokai.or.jp	
KENYA	EAN – Executive Assistant Network	www.payaafrica.org	Winnie Kamuya
KENYA	IRC – International Renaissance Centre	www.irc@arcafrica.org	Winnie Kamuya
KOREA	ASA – Association of Secretaries and Administrative Professionals in Asia Pacific	www.asapap.org	Lilian Coloma (ASA General Secretary)
LUXEMBOURG	IMA Luxembourg	www.lu.ima-network.org	Catherine Johansson – Chairman

MALAYSIA	MAPSA – Malaysian Association of Professional Secretaries & Administrators	www.mapsa-malaysia.com	Sylvia Thomas
MIDDLE EAST	CIPD, Middle East (Chartered Institute of Personnel and Development)	www.cipd.ae	Ricky Araujo
NETHERLANDS	IMA, Netherlands	www.nl.ima-network.org	Greetje van Vroonhoven-Mensing – Chairman
NETHERLANDS	NVD – Nederlandse Vereniging van Directiesecretaressen	www.nvdsecretaresse.nl	Annelies Bessels
NEW ZEALAND	AAPNZ – Association of Administrative Professionals New Zealand Inc	www.aapnz.org.nz	Alison McKessar – National President

NEW ZEALAND	AAPNZ Auckland – Association of Administrative Professionals New Zealand Inc	www.aapnz.org.nz/auckland.aspx	Joss Drummond
NEW ZEALAND	AAPNZ Christchurch – Association of Administrative Professionals New Zealand Inc	www.aapnz.org.nz/christchurch.aspx	Joanne Gallop
NEW ZEALAND	AAPNZ Dunedin – Association of Administrative Professionals New Zealand Inc	www.aapnz.org.nz/dunedin/aspx	Tracey Fleet
NEW ZEALAND	AAPNZ Waikato – Association of Administrative Professionals New Zealand Inc	www.aapnz.org.nz/hamilton/aspx	Viv Thorpe
NEW ZEALAND	AAPNZ Manawatu – Association of Administrative Professionals New Zealand Inc	www.aapnz.org.nz/manawatu/aspx	Kath Olliver
NEW ZEALAND	AAPNZ Marlborough – Association of Administrative Professionals New Zealand Inc	www.aapnz.org.nz/marlborough/aspx	Jane Ingram

Country	Organization	Website	Contact
NEW ZEALAND	AAPNZ Nelson – Association of Administrative Professionals New Zealand Inc	www.aapnz.org.nz/nelson.aspx	Shelley Hawke
NEW ZEALAND	AAPNZ Rotorua – Association of Administrative Professionals New Zealand Inc	www.aapnz.org.nz/rotorua/aspz	Tracey Kerr
NEW ZEALAND	AAPNZ Tauranga – Association of Administrative Professionals New Zealand Inc	www.aapnz.org.nz/tuaranga/aspx	Tracy Sherlock
NEW ZEALAND	AAPNZ Wellington – Association of Administrative Professionals New Zealand Inc	www.aapnz.org.nz/wellington/aspx	Dianne Parker
NEW ZEALAND	AAPNZ Whanganui – Association of Administrative Professionals New Zealand Inc	www.aapnz.org.nz/whanganui/aspx	Veronica Stevens
NEW ZEALAND	PACE – Professional Assistants to Chief Executives	www.pace.org.nz	Rebecca Dobbs
			Nicky Andrew
NORWAY	IMA, Norway	www.no.ima-network.org	Julia Schmidt – Chairman

PAKISTAN	Distinguished Secretaries' Society of Pakistan (DSSP)	www.dssp.org	Natasha Mavalvala
PANAMA	Asociacion de Secretarias Ejecutivas de Panama		Lic Marla Hernandez U – President
PHILIPPINES	Philippine Association of Secretaries and Administrative Professionals	www.philsecretaries.org	Under construction
PORTUGAL	ASP – Associacã de Secretarias Profissionais Portuguesas	www.asp-secretarias.pt	Maria da Graca Gomes
RUSSIA	IMA, Russia	www.ru.ima-network.org	Olga Gorina – Chairman
RUSSIA	The National Association of Office specialists and administrative staff	www.center-expert.org	Lyudmila Petrovna
SINGAPORE	SAAP – Singapore Association of Administrative Professionals	www.saap.org.sg	
SOUTH AFRICA	PAN-SA – Platinum Assistant Network in South Africa	www.platinumassistsa.org.za	Cathy Harris Michele Thwaits Susan Engelbrecht

SPAIN	ASPA – Asociacion del Secretariado Profesional de Aragon	www.asparagon.com	
SPAIN	ASPM – Asociación del Secretariado Profesional de Madrid	www.aspm.es	
SPAIN	IMA, Spain	www.es.ima-network.org	Anna M Hueto – Chairman
SPAIN	SEIEM – Secretariat i Empresa	www.secretariatiempresa.blogspot.com	
SRI LANKA	Sri Lanka Association of Administrative & Professional Secretaries	www.slaapsonline.com	Ruveena Cader
SWEDEN	Chefssekreterarna Stockholm (Chefs Assistants)	www.cssto.se	No Callersjo (Chairman)
SWEDEN	IMA, Sweden	www.se.ima-network.org	Helena Moren – Chairperson IMA North
			Theres Westrin – Chairperson IMA East
			Carina Frickeus – Chairperson IMA West

SWITZERLAND	IMA, Switzerland	www.ch.ima-network.org	Karin Helene – Chairperson IMA South Kelly-Jayne Dulex – Chairman
SWITZERLAND	Miss Moneypenny	www.missmoneypenny.ch	Isabella Cottone
TAIWAN	CASAP – Republic of China Professional Secretarial cum Executives Association	www.chinesesecretary.org.tw	
THAILAND	Women Secretaries Association of Thailand (WSAT)	www.secretarythailand.org	
TURKEY	IMA, Turkey	www.tr.ima-network.org	Menekse Ahbab – Chairman
UGANDA	NASAP – National Association of Secretaries and Administrative Professionals	www.nasapuganda.org	Harriet Nabirye
UNITED ARAB EMIRATES	Platinum PA Club	www.platinumpaclub.com	Warsha Joshi Seema Ramchand
UNITED KINGDOM	ACA – Association of Celebrity Assistants	www.aca-uk.com	Yonel Osman (Events)

UNITED KINGDOM	AMSPAR – Association of Medical Secretaries, Practice Managers, Administrators & Receptionists	www.amspar.com	Tom Brownlie
UNITED KINGDOM	Berkshire & North Hants PA Network	www.berksnorthhants panetwork.wordpress. com	Karen
UNITED KINGDOM	Bristol PA Network	www.bristolpanetwork. co.uk	Debs Eden
UNITED KINGDOM	British Society of Medical Secretaries & Administrators (BSMSA)	www.bsmsa.org.uk	Liz Wilson
UNITED KINGDOM	Bucks PA Network	www.buckspanetwork. co.uk	Sarah Howson
UNITED KINGDOM	Cardiff PA Network (Wales)	www.cardiffpanetwork. com	Catrin Morgan
UNITED KINGDOM	Charity PA Network	No Website Address	Leeanne Graham
UNITED KINGDOM	CIPD, UK (Chartered Institute of Personnel and Development)	www.cipd.co.uk	

UNITED KINGDOM	EPAA – Executive and Personal Assistants Association Ltd	www.epaa.org.uk	Victoria Darragh
UNITED KINGDOM	Executive VPA	www.executivevpa.co.uk	
UNITED KINGDOM	Exeter PA Network	www.exeterpanetwork.com	Kim Glover & Rebecca Eccles
UNITED KINGDOM	Forum Exents – UK	www.forumevents.co.uk	
UNITED KINGDOM	IAgSA – Institute of Agricultural Secretaries & Administrators	www.iagsa.co.uk	
UNITED KINGDOM	IMA, UK	www.uk.ima-network.org	Elizabeth Wakeling – Chairman
UNITED KINGDOM	Lanarkshire PA Network	www.lanarkshirepanetwork.co.uk	Kelly McAulay
UNITED KINGDOM	LCCI PA Club	www.londonchamber.co.uk/lcc_public/article.asp?aid=1213	Jan Mackay, Florent Dupriez

UNITED KINGDOM	London City Airport Premier PA Club	www.londoncityairport.com/premierpa	Anne Marks
UNITED KINGDOM	London PA Network	www.london-pa-network.org	Melanie Sheehy
			Amanda Hargreaves
UNITED KINGDOM	Manchester PA Network	www.manchesterpanetwork.co.uk	Emily Darnell
			Esther Dawson
UNITED KINGDOM	Miss Jones PA	www.missjonespa.com	Paula van Straten
UNITED KINGDOM	National Association for Legal Assistants	www.nala.org	Angela Garry
UNITED KINGDOM	National Association of Headteachers' PAs (NAHPA)	www.nahpa.org.uk	Julia Robertson
			Karen Glenn

UNITED KINGDOM	Newcastle PA Network	www.newcastlepanetwork.com	Gina Antoniou
UNITED KINGDOM	North London VA Network	www.paworkstation.co.uk	Victoria Norris & Emily Mills
UNITED KINGDOM	Number 42	www.number-42.com	Elaine Jones
UNITED KINGDOM	Oxford PA Network	www.oxfordpanetwork.co.uk	Merryl Futerman and Josephine Green
UNITED KINGDOM	PA Access All Areas	www.paaccessallareas.co.uk	Kerry Hammond, Marion White
UNITED KINGDOM	PA Network Hull & Humber	www.panetwork.co.uk	John Palmer
UNITED KINGDOM	PA-Assist.com	www.pa-assist.com	Marguerita King
UNITED KINGDOM	Personal Assistant Tips.com	www.personal-assistant-tips.com	Bethany Fovargue
UNITED KINGDOM	Plymouth PA Network	www.plymouthpanetwork.co.uk	Nicky Christmas

UNITED KINGDOM	PPPA – Practically Perfect PA	www.practicallyperfectpa.com	Caroline Wylie
UNITED KINGDOM	Scottish PA Network (Scotland)	www.scottishpanetwork.com	Rosemary McLennan
UNITED KINGDOM	Society of Virtual Assistants (SVA)	www.societyofvirtualassistants.co.uk	Helen Rees
UNITED KINGDOM	Supporting Professionals Network Leeds Beckett	www.leedsbeckett.ac.uk/staffing/supporting-professionals-network.htm	
UNITED KINGDOM	The Asssistant Room	www.theassistantroom.com	Jessice Gardiner
UNITED KINGDOM	The Cambridge Network PA Forum	www.cambridgenetwork.co.uk/learning/peer-learning	Victoria Darragh
UNITED KINGDOM	The Executive & Personal Assistants Association	www.epaa.org.uk	Emma Stacey
UNITED KINGDOM	The Institute of Administrative Management	www.instam.org	Andrew Jardine

UNITED KINGDOM	The Institute of Legal Secretaries and PAs	www.institutelegalsecretaries.com	Ayesha Nicholls
UNITED KINGDOM	The PA Club	www.thepaclub.com	Marion Lowrence
UNITED KINGDOM	The PA Hub	www.thepahub.co.uk	Athena Caramitsos – Corp events
			Alison Paton – PA Network
UNITED KINGDOM	The PA Network (City Co)	www.cityco.com/project/the-pa-network/	Alison Paton – PA Network
UNITED KINGDOM	We are the City	www.wearethecity.com	Debbie Apted
UNITED KINGDOM	Weston-super-Mare PA Network	www.westonchamber.org.uk	Rosemary Parr
UK, EUROPE, MIDDLE EAST, FAR EAST, AUSTRALIA	Global PA Association	www.globalpa-association.com	

UNITED STATES	ACPA – Association of Celebrity Personal Assistants, Los Angeles	www.acpa-la.com	Lisa Olsen
UNITED STATES	Admin to Admin	www.admintoadmin.net	
UNITED STATES	Adminpro	www.adminprotoday.com	
UNITED STATES	AEAP – Association of Executive & Administrative Professionals	www.theaeap.com	Terry Thompson
UNITED STATES	AHCAP – Association for Healthcare Administrative Professionals	www.ahcap.org	Peggy Vasquez
UNITED STATES	APTC – Administrative Professionals of the Tri-Cities	www.adminprofessionalstc.org	Grace Brown
UNITED STATES	ASAP – American Society of Administrative Professionals	www.asaporg.com	Debbi Shaffer
UNITED STATES	Audacious Admin	www.audaciousadmin.com	Loretta Sophocleous, President

UNITED STATES	C-Suite Executive Support Professionals	www.C-SESP.org	William Richardson
UNITED STATES	IAAP – International Association of Administrative Professional s	www.iaap-hq.org	Rachel Reynolds
UNITED STATES	IAPO – International Association of Professional Assistants	www.iapcollege.com	
UNITED STATES	IVAA – International Virtual Assistants Association	www.ivaa.org	
UNITED STATES	Legal Secretaries International Inc	www.legalsecretaries.org	Kelly Engstrom, President
UNITED STATES	National Association for Legal Assistants	www.nala.org	Paula van Straten
UNITED STATES	New York Celebrity Assistants	www.nycelebrityassistants.com	
UNITED STATES	Office Ninjas	www.officeninjas.com	Nikki Holland
UNITED STATES	Office Team – a Robert Half Company	www.officeteam.com	Cynthia Kong

UNITED STATES	The PA Network (Jersey)	www.thepanetworkjersey.com	Karen Porter
UNITED STATES	Virtual Association for Administrative Professionals	www.thevaap.com	
URUGUAY	ADESU – Associación de Secretarias del Uruguay	www.adesu.org.uy	Victoria Rabin
USA	EAO – Executive Assistants Organisaton	www.executiveassistantsorganization.com	Catrin Morgan
ZIMBABWE	ICSAZ – Institute of Charrered Secretaries and Administrators	www.icsaz.co.zw	

About the Author

Cathy Harris has been part of the Discovery Internal Assistant Network since 2001. She was instrumental in the initial stages of its creation, its growth and continued success, and served as Chairperson on various occasions. The Discovery Internal Network went through a period of change early in 2015, and the Assistant Forum was renamed the Discovery Centre of Excellence; an apt name for a formidable force of assistants.

Cathy was nominated for and awarded the title of South African National Secretary of the Year in 2006. It became her objective and ambition to develop the secretarial profession, in order for assistants to be recognized as strategic partners with the leadership that they support.

She is currently the Executive Assistant to the CEO of Discovery Invest, which is part of Discovery Holdings, a shared value insurance company whose purpose and ambition are achieved through a pioneering business model that incentivizes people to be healthier, and enhances and protects their lives. It is a forward-thinking and innovative organization, and with this in mind, the assistants who support this leadership also share the same value and spirit.

Cathy has been in the secretarial profession for over 36 years, and admits that she has gained a wealth of knowledge, wisdom, skill and inspiration from her fellow peers, who have inspired her to innovate and sustain the Discovery Assistant Centre of Excellence initiatives.

Index

21722982R00079

Printed in Great Britain
by Amazon